JOURNEYI.   ... THE YEAR OF LUKE

JOURNEYING THROUGH THE YEAR OF LUKE

Reflections on the Gospel

John Littleton

⊕

Published 2009 by Veritas Publications
7–8 Lower Abbey Street
Dublin 1, Ireland
publications@veritas.ie
www.veritas.ie

ISBN 978 1 84730 206 9

10 9 8 7 6 5 4 3 2 1

A catalogue record for this book is available from the
British Library.

Printed in the Republic of Ireland by Hudson Killeen,
Dublin.

*Veritas books are printed on paper made from the wood
pulp of managed forests. For every tree felled, at least one
tree is planted, thereby renewing natural resources.*

CONTENTS ⊕

Holy Days and Some Other Feasts

PREFACE ⊕

The Gospel is Good News. The purpose of this book is to provide readers with an overview of the Gospel according to Luke, which is proclaimed during Year C of the Church's liturgical cycle. After introducing the principal themes of Luke's Gospel, a series of reflections on the gospel readings is presented for each Sunday and major feast during the year.

The reflections focus on the relevance of Luke's Gospel for everyday life and will be helpful to priests and laity wishing to engage more fully with the word of God. An appendix at the end of the book indicates the order for the gospel readings in Ordinary time.

The reflections form the substantial part of the book. Before each one, the reference for the relevant gospel reading is listed. Then after each reflection, a suitable phrase or short passage from the gospel is offered as an aid to personal prayer and meditation.

The scripture quotations throughout the book are taken from the *Jerusalem Bible* because that is the version of the scriptures that is generally used in lectionaries and, as such, the version with which most people are familiar.

While the reflections may be read without necessarily referring to the gospel texts, it is recommended that readers also use their Bibles or missals. Otherwise, individual gospel phrases could be taken out of context. Also, because the word of God is inexhaustible, it is impossible to be totally comprehensive in any given reflection. Hopefully, the reflections presented here will inspire readers to develop their own thoughts on the Gospel of Luke.

Finally, earlier versions of some of the reflections were published in *The Catholic Times* and in the *Tipperary Star*.

I: INTRODUCING THE GOSPEL ACCORDING TO LUKE

✠

GOD'S PROMISE TO SEND ⊕
THE MESSIAH IS FULFILLED
IN JESUS OF NAZARETH

GOSPEL AND GOOD NEWS

The English word 'gospel' is derived from an older expression meaning 'glad tidings' which, in turn, translates the Greek term for 'good news'. Christians believe that the Gospel is the Good News of salvation, which acknowledges and proclaims that Jesus of Nazareth is the Son of God and the Saviour of the world.

This news is indeed good because it assures Christians that, through his suffering, death and resurrection, Jesus conquered the power of sin and restored integrity to the relationship between God and the human race that had been damaged by sin. The Good News continues to be announced to the farthest ends of the earth by Jesus' disciples in his Church, so that every generation may experience the saving power of the risen Lord.

The canon (that is, the rule) of scripture, which lists the authoritative books in the Bible, recognises four gospels: those of Matthew, Mark, Luke and John. Each of the four evangelists (that is, in this technical instance, those who are attributed with having written the gospels)[1] presents a particular understanding of the life and ministry of Jesus the Messiah. That understanding is influenced by several factors, including the evangelist's knowledge and personal experience of Jesus, the precise context in which he writes, and the spiritual concerns and needs of the audience for which he is writing.

ONE GOSPEL, FOUR GOSPELS

Fundamentally, then, there are four presentations of the same Good News, albeit with different purposes and emphases. That is why, for example, it is more accurate to describe the 'Gospel of Luke' as the 'Gospel according to Luke', in the sense that it is essentially the Good News of salvation being communicated from Luke's perspective. This is evident from the prescribed introduction to the gospel reading during the celebration of the Eucharist, when the priest or deacon announces: 'A reading from the Holy Gospel according to Luke.'

The gospels of Matthew, Mark and Luke – as distinct from that of John – have many similarities in style, structure and content, which are obvious from the various incidents and teachings of Jesus that are common to all three.[2] In contrast, John presents Jesus and his ministry quite differently. Nevertheless, it has been the Church's consistent teaching that, regardless of individual differences and distinctive features, the gospels – like all the other books in the Bible – are divinely inspired. They are the word of God.

LUKE THE EVANGELIST

Luke, who is not identified by name in his gospel, was probably a Gentile Christian. He was a citizen of Antioch, the capital of Syria, and a physician.[3] It is generally agreed that Luke did not witness Jesus' ministry directly, but that he was a disciple and companion of the Apostle to the Gentiles, Paul (see Colossians 4:4, 2 Timothy 4:11 and Philemon 24). Luke incorporated some of Paul's teachings with the other sources (see Luke 1:1-3), including the Gospel of Mark, that he used when writing his gospel. On reading Luke, it quickly becomes clear that he was a good narrator and, from the many parables recorded, an excellent storyteller.

The Gospel according to Luke

The Gospel according to Luke, written in Greek, is the longest of the four gospels and it records the life and ministry of Jesus from his miraculous conception and birth to his ascension into heaven. Jesus' ministry was characterised by preaching – especially in parables – and healing miracles. He was gentle, in the sense of being compassionate to those in need, but demanded total commitment from his disciples, in the sense of taking up their cross every day and renouncing their possessions (see Luke 14:25-33).

While Luke's Gospel is fundamentally concerned with Jesus' message of salvation, this is manifested especially by Jesus' concern for the poor, the sick and afflicted, and outcasts. Women were significant in Jesus' ministry. The gospel emphasises the ongoing work of the Holy Spirit, the prayer of Jesus, and the joy of being in a life-giving relationship with God.[4]

The contents of Luke's Gospel may be divided into six sections:
1. The preface (see Luke 1:1-4).
2. The birth and infancy narratives (see Luke 1:5–2:52).
3. The Galilean ministry (see Luke 3:1–9:50).

4. The journey to Jerusalem through Samaria
   (see Luke 9:51–19:48).
5. The Jerusalem ministry (see Luke 20–21).
6. The passion and resurrection narrative
   (see Luke 22–24).

The fulfilment of God's promise to send the Messiah, in Jesus of Nazareth, is Luke's central theme (see Luke 4:21 and 24:44-53). Although Jesus' ministry ended in apparent failure, when he died on the cross, he was vindicated by the Father when he rose from the dead. In Jesus, God brought salvation to his people.[5]

GOOD NEWS FOR THE GENTILES

Unlike Matthew, who wrote his gospel mainly for a Jewish-Christian community, Luke wrote from a predominantly Gentile perspective and, like Mark, primarily for a Gentile-Christian community. Luke's essential message is that God's salvation is universal and inclusive. It is not confined exclusively to the Jews, but is available to all people. The majority of biblical scholars now agree that Luke wrote his gospel some years after the destruction of the Temple in AD 70,[6] probably as late as AD 80–85.

Luke wrote his gospel so that his readers would 'know how well founded the teaching [was] that [they had] received' (Luke 1:4). The implication is that Luke knew that his readers were already familiar with the person and teaching of Jesus. So Luke's desire was to confirm his readers in their existing faith and to develop further their understanding of the Good News of salvation and their commitment to Jesus.

Using contemporary terminology, we could say that Luke was engaging in catechesis, not evangelisation.[7] This has relevance for contemporary Christians who are celebrating the Year of Luke because, like Luke's intended audience, we already know Jesus and his message. Thus our purpose in journeying through the Year of Luke is to develop further our Christian faith by deepening our commitment to Jesus and appreciating the salvation he won for us.

THE SIGNIFICANCE OF JERUSALEM

Luke also wrote the Acts of the Apostles. Luke's Gospel and Acts could be described a two-part work. His gospel deals with the life, death and resurrection of Jesus whereas Acts begins with the ascension and describes the spread of the early Church. Significantly, the Gospel begins and ends in Jerusalem. Acts also begins in Jerusalem, with the early Church subsequently spreading from there. Journeys to and from that city are central to both writings.

The focus of Jesus' entire ministry was directed towards Jerusalem as is stated several times by Luke: 'now as the time drew near for [Jesus] to be taken up to heaven, he resolutely took the road for Jerusalem' (Luke 9:51), and 'through towns and villages [Jesus] went teaching, making his way to Jerusalem' (Luke 13:22), and 'now on the way to Jerusalem [Jesus] travelled along the border between Samaria and Galilee' (Luke 17:11). Jerusalem was the city of destiny for him because it was there that salvation would be achieved (see Luke 13:31-35).

Both the Gospel according to Luke and the Acts of the Apostles are addressed to Theophilus (meaning, in Greek, a friend of God) who was an important person in the society of the day. We know this because Luke addresses him as 'Your Excellency' (Luke 1:4). He was obviously a supporter of Luke and, perhaps, a benefactor. It is possible that Theophilus requested Luke to write an account of Jesus' life and ministry.

There are several passages in Luke's Gospel that are not found in the other gospels. They include:

- The accounts of the annunciation (see Luke 1:26-38), the visitation of Elizabeth (see Luke 1:39-56), Mary's Magnificat (see Luke 1:46-55), the presentation of Jesus in the Temple (see Luke 2:22-38) and the finding of Jesus in the Temple (see Luke 2:41-50).
- The restoration to life of the son of the widow of Nain (see Luke 7:11-17).
- Jesus' encounter with the woman who washed and anointed his feet (see Luke 7:36-50).
- The mission of the seventy-two disciples (see Luke 10:1-20).
- The parable of the good Samaritan (see Luke 10:29-37).
- Jesus' visit to the home of Martha and Mary (see Luke 10:38-42).
- The parable of the importunate (that is, persistent) friend (see Luke 11:5-8).
- The parable of the rich fool (see Luke 12:13-21).
- The parables of the lost drachma, the lost sheep and the prodigal son (see Luke 15:1-32).
- The parables of the unjust steward (see Luke 16:1-13) and the rich man and Lazarus (see Luke 16:19-31).
- The healing of the ten lepers (see Luke 17:11-19).
- The parables of the unscrupulous judge (see Luke 18:1-8) and the Pharisee and the publican (see Luke 18:9-14).
- Jesus' visit to the house of Zacchaeus (see Luke 19:1-10).
- The encounter between Jesus and the repentant thief on Calvary (see Luke 23:35-43).

THE ACTIVITY OF THE HOLY SPIRIT

The influence of the Holy Spirit is evident throughout Luke's Gospel. For example, John the Baptist was 'filled with the Holy Spirit' (Luke 1:15) in the presence of Jesus. Jesus himself was conceived by the power of the Spirit (see Luke 1:35) and 'the Holy Spirit descended on him' (Luke 3:22) after his baptism before leading him into the wilderness (see Luke 4:1) where he was tempted by the Devil. As he began his public ministry in Galilee, Jesus stated that the Spirit had been given to him (see Luke 4:18) to accompany him in his ministry. Then, at the end of his earthly ministry, Jesus promised his apostles that he would send them the Holy Spirit to help them to be witnesses to God's salvation (see Luke 24:49).

SALVATION IS FOR EVERYONE WHO REPENTS, NOT ONLY THE JEWS

The context in which Luke wrote his gospel was that of the Jews rejecting Jesus as the Messiah. Early in his ministry, Jesus had prophesied that the religious leaders would persuade the Jews not to accept him and his message of salvation when he said that the Son of Man would be 'rejected by the elders and chief priests and scribes' (Luke 9:22).

Therefore, God's salvation is universal. It is a gift from God, freely offered to all people who repent for their sins and accept Jesus as their Lord and Saviour. In other words, it is offered to Jews and Gentiles alike. An indication of this is found in Luke's genealogy of Jesus, which traces Jesus' ancestry back to Adam, the father of all human beings (see Luke 3:23-38), thereby relating Jesus to every human being – unlike Matthew who traces Jesus' ancestry back to Abraham thus linking him only with Abraham's descendants. Likewise, the new children of Abraham are those who accept the salvation offered by Jesus (see Luke 19:9) rather than those who are simply descended from Abraham.

Luke's message is unambiguous: everyone is important to Jesus. He is even 'a light to enlighten the pagans' (Luke 2:32). This is obvious in the parable about the man hosting a great banquet who said to his servant: 'Go to the open roads and the hedgerows and force people to come in to make sure my house is full' (Luke 14:23). It is also evident from Jesus' final instruction to his apostles: 'in [Christ's] name, repentance for the forgiveness of sins would be preached to all the nations, beginning from Jerusalem' (Luke 24:47).

CONCERN FOR ALL THOSE WHO ARE VULNERABLE

In the Gospel according to Luke, Jesus constantly demonstrates his concern for women, children, the sick, the poor, outsiders, foreigners and especially sinners. Through his many parables and various healing miracles, he proves that he is a friend to everyone in need: 'for the Son of Man has come to seek out and save what was lost' (Luke 19:10).

Jesus' compassion is clearly demonstrated in his respectful dealing with the repentant woman (see Luke 7:36-50), his parable about patience with the barren fig tree (see Luke 13:6-9) and especially his response to the good thief (see Luke 23:39-43). His attention to those who were classified as outcasts is evident in his treatment of the ten lepers (see Luke 17:11-19) and in his respect for the Samaritans.

Examples of Jesus' attitude towards the poor and his challenge to help those who are poor are found in the parable of the rich fool (see Luke 12:13-21), his instruction to invite the poor to banquets (see Luke 14:12-14) and the parable of the rich man and Lazarus (see Luke 16:19-31). Jesus addressed the beatitudes to the poor while addressing the curses towards the rich (see Luke 6:20-26). The poor always had a special place in Jesus' heart.

Prayer

Jesus' ability to respond to the needs of those around him and to focus his attention on those who were considered unimportant was undoubtedly based on his close relationship with his heavenly Father. This was expressed and deepened through the time he spent in prayer. From reading Luke's Gospel, we know that prayer was the central activity in Jesus' life and that he always prayed at crucial times during his ministry, including:

- Prior to choosing the twelve apostles (see Luke 6:12).
- Before being transfigured in the presence of Peter, John and James (see Luke 9:28).
- Prior to being arrested and sentenced to death (see Luke 22:41).
- Shortly before dying on the cross (see Luke 23:34, 46).

In Jesus' preaching, he emphasised the necessity of prayer for his disciples, especially in the parable of the importunate friend (see Luke 11:5-13), the parable of the unscrupulous judge (see Luke 18:1-8) and the parable of the Pharisee and the publican (see Luke 18:9-14). Jesus challenged his disciples to become praying people when he taught them how to pray (see Luke 11:1-13).

Significance of women

In Luke's Gospel, great prominence is given to women and their role in Jesus' ministry. There are more women in Luke's Gospel than in the others. In Jewish society, women did not have the same social and legal status as men. Luke's Gospel challenges that practice. Among the women are:
- Mary, the mother of Jesus, the first disciple, who pondered the word of God (see Luke 2:19).

- Elizabeth, the cousin of Mary and the mother of John the Baptist (see Luke 1:39-58).
- Anna, the prophetess (see Luke 2:36-38).
- The widow of Nain (see Luke 7:11-17).
- The woman who was a sinner (see Luke 7:36-50).
- Certain women from Galilee who accompanied Jesus during his public ministry: Mary Magdalene, Joanna, Susanna and several others (see Luke 8:2-3).
- The sisters Martha and Mary (see Luke 10:38-42).
- The woman in the crowd who praised the mother of Jesus (see Luke 11:27).
- The woman in the parable of the lost drachma (see Luke 15:8-10).
- The woman in the parable of the unscrupulous judge (see Luke 18:1-8).
- The women of Jerusalem who mourned and lamented for Jesus on the way to Calvary (see Luke 23:27-31).
- The women from Galilee who came to Jesus' tomb with spices and ointment to care for his dead body (see Luke 23:55).
- The women who are the first witnesses of the resurrection (see Luke 24:8-11).

JOYFULNESS

The Gospel according to Luke is characterised by a spirit of joy which, in turn, is the joy of the Holy Spirit. The arrival of God's salvation brings joy. Several examples of rejoicing are to be found throughout the gospel:

- The baby in Elizabeth's womb leapt for joy in the presence of the Messiah (see Luke 1:44).
- Mary, the mother of Jesus, praises God in joy (see Luke 1:46-55).

- The angel has 'news of great joy' (Luke 2:10) for the shepherds, that is to be shared by the whole people.
- During his public ministry, Jesus urges his disciples to 'rejoice that your names are written in heaven' (Luke 10:20).
- Jesus was 'filled with joy by the Holy Spirit' (Luke 10:21).
- The parables of the lost sheep (see Luke 15:4-7), the lost drachma (see Luke 15:8-10) and the prodigal son (see Luke 15:11-32) all end with a great sense of rejoicing.
- Zacchaeus 'welcomed [Jesus] joyfully' (Luke 19:6) to his house.
- After Jesus ascended to heaven, the apostles 'went back to Jerusalem full of joy' (Luke 24:52).

LUKE IN RELIGIOUS ART AND IN POPULAR DEVOTION

In religious art, Luke is traditionally represented by a bull. This is based on a text from Revelation: 'In the centre, grouped round the throne itself, were four animals with many eyes, in front and behind. The first animal was like a lion, the second like a bull, the third animal had a human face, and the fourth animal was like a flying eagle (Revelation 4:6-7).

Each of the four evangelists is often represented by one of the four animals. Mark is usually represented by a lion. Matthew is frequently depicted by a human face. John is normally portrayed as a flying eagle. And Luke is regularly symbolised by a bull. However, there are also other representations of Luke in religious iconography. For example, one of the earliest images of Luke is of him sitting at a desk painting a picture of Mary the mother of Jesus.

In terms of popular devotion, physicians and surgeons espouse Luke as their patron saint. Butchers have adopted Luke as their patron saint because of the image of the bull that is used to depict him. Not surprisingly, artists have also adopted Luke as their patron saint because of the tradition that he painted an icon of Mary and because of the many inspiring word pictures that are part of his narrative style. Luke's feast is celebrated on 18 October each year.

NOTES

1. In contemporary usage, the term 'evangelist' has a wider meaning than simply a writer of one of the four gospels. It is generally used to refer to people who preach and publicise the Good News, which is the word of God.

2. Because of their similarities, the gospels of Matthew, Mark and Luke are collectively known as the synoptic gospels.

3. Paul describes him as his 'dear friend, Luke, the doctor' (Colossians 4:14).

4. Relevant examples of each category are provided in later sections of this essay.

5. The name 'Jesus' means 'God saves'.

6. See Luke 21:5-30 for Jesus' prediction that the Temple would be destroyed.

7. There is a distinction between evangelisation and catechesis. Evangelisation attempts to awaken faith, and occurs when people are first introduced to the person of Jesus and to his teaching. In contrast, catechesis presumes some level of pre-existing faith that may be further developed. So evangelisation occurs prior to catechesis.

II: REFLECTIONS

⊕

THE PROPER OF SEASONS ⊕

The Season of Advent
⊕
First Sunday of Advent

GOSPEL READING: LUKE 21:25-28, 34-36

REFLECTION

The word Advent, from the Latin *adventus*, means 'an arrival' or 'a coming'. Specifically for Christians, the arrival or coming to which we refer is the arrival of Jesus Christ, the Messiah, our Lord and Saviour. He is the perfect fulfilment of God's plan for our salvation. The liturgical season of Advent focuses on our waiting for his glorious arrival at the end of time. But it also focuses on our recalling the many centuries for which God's people waited before the Messiah's birth in Bethlehem more than two thousand years ago.

As Advent begins, we are invited to embrace the sense of waiting for Christ's arrival. Advent is about waiting and we are the people who are waiting. However, if our waiting is not to become tedious and futile then it needs to be purposeful. Thus we are encouraged to use properly our time-of-waiting by preparing in hope and expectation for Christ who is coming.

The word of God teaches us that, if our waiting is not to be in vain, we need to stay awake because we do not know precisely when Christ will come. He often comes when we least expect him. This is particularly true regarding the moment of death for many people. Hence it is necessary to remain attentive and alert while preparing to meet him in life and in death. This involves listening and watching for him so that we do not miss his arrival. We do this by preparing our souls for God's judgement as we do penance in atonement for our sins.

Paradoxically, while we wait for Jesus our Saviour to come to us – whether at the end of our earthly lives and the end of time, or as we commemorate his birth in Bethlehem – he is here already. We meet him in word and in sacrament, especially as he shares his life with us in a unique way whenever we celebrate the Eucharist. We also meet him in the encouraging and hopeful words spoken to us by other people when, for instance, we are disillusioned, broken-hearted or depressed. We meet him in the sadness of those whose lives have been devastated by violence, illness and grief. And we meet Jesus in the Church and its teaching because the Church is the Body of Christ.

So our waiting for the Lord's coming is not in a vacuum. During Advent, we remember the centuries of waiting for the fulfilment of God's promise to send the Saviour. We remind ourselves that we are awaiting his glorious return at the end of time. Nevertheless, the Saviour is here already. But unless we stay awake and alert, listening for his word and watching for the signs of his presence, we will not recognise him as he enters our lives. If we do not familiarise ourselves with him now, how will we recognise him when he comes at the moment of death? The season of Advent provides us with the opportunity to wait for the Lord's arrival by rejecting sin and by preparing our hearts and lives to accept him when he comes.

FOR MEDITATION
Your liberation is near at hand. (LUKE 21:28)

⊕
Second Sunday of Advent

GOSPEL READING: LUKE 3:1-6

REFLECTION
John the Baptist was the herald chosen by God to prepare the way for Christ. The call to abandon sin and become repentant was central to his preaching. Prior to his ministry, he spent time in the wilderness because he knew that penance and conversion were necessary as he prepared for the Messiah's arrival.

Retreating from the hustle and bustle of everyday life and seeking prayerful silence is essential if we are to discern God's will as it challenges us to obey the commandments and to be free from sin. Being in the wilderness, regardless of how we discover and experience it, when used constructively, fosters the deepening of holiness because it is where we truly encounter God.

We observe from John's preaching that the word of God was his most prized possession. God's word taught him that God's promise to send the Messiah would indeed be realised. John subsequently shared that consoling and challenging message with the people, hoping that they would respond as he had responded. He was a strong, prophetic figure who provided an example of how we need not be afraid to confront the evils of our time.

John's witnessing was so dramatic and convincing that many people would have been happy to follow him and declare their allegiance to him. Yet, for all of his influence and the possibilities of establishing himself as their spiritual leader, he insisted that he was preparing the way for someone much more significant than him: the Messiah. He obviously believed that he could not be deflected from his main task through being fooled by the short-term adulation offered by his listeners.

The season of Advent invites us to be credible and courageous witnesses to the Good News. We are encouraged to avoid the danger of becoming arrogant by promoting our own name and fame instead of the name and power of Jesus Christ. Then other people will notice our prophetic lifestyles in a rapidly expanding secular world. Just as John the Baptist provided a suitable opportunity for Christ to come into people's lives without confusing them between himself and Christ, we do the same. John preached the truth because God had decreed that human beings would be saved by the truth.

During Advent we are encouraged to spend time in silence discerning God's will and the Church's teaching. We reflect on what we believe to be our most prized possession and we check whether or not it is compatible with the word of God. We generously share Christ's consoling and challenging message with the people we meet. And we courageously witness to the teaching of Christ and his Church by the sincerity of our convictions.

As Christians, our lifestyle is meant to be different from those around us who are not Christian. If John the Baptist worked alongside us, would he, for example, hear us swearing or see us being uncharitable? And if he did, would he turn a deaf ear or a blind eye?

Many of us are reluctant to speak about our faith and share it with others. The challenge of the Good News is to become humble disciples, always permitting the name and power of Jesus Christ to take precedence over our own name and fame. Like John the Baptist, we are called to be people of hope and expectation awaiting the coming of Christ at Christmas and at the moment of death.

FOR MEDITATION

And all mankind shall see the salvation of God.
(LUKE 3:6)

⊕
Third Sunday of Advent

GOSPEL READING: LUKE 3:10-18

REFLECTION

A sensible way to prepare for Christ's arrival is to learn from the example of other people who have prepared well while they awaited his arrival. There are many such examples in the Bible and John the Baptist is one of the dominant and most striking.

John's preparation for the Messiah's arrival was characterised by his preaching. He preached a message of hope and repentance to dejected people – whose land was occupied by foreigners, who were often exploited by their religious leaders and who had become spiritually enslaved to sin. John also fasted and did penance in preparation for the coming of the long-awaited Messiah and he urged other people to do the same.

John learnt that the only way to become disentangled from sin is through repentance and conversion. Thus his preaching focused on the urgency of repentance and he reassured the people about God's providential care and complete fidelity towards them even when, at times, they were unfaithful and sinful. They could be certain that God's promise to send the Saviour would soon be realised.

We are asked to emulate John's example by being people who are repentant for our sins. We are invited to encourage other people to become repentant too. Christ and sin are incompatible. We cannot truly meet Christ as he comes into our lives each day unless we are without sin because it imprisons us and prevents us from recognising him.

Nowadays, many people have lost their sense of sin. They mistakenly think that sin does not exist. They presume that they can do whatever they wish. In effect, God gave us free will so that we can choose good instead of evil. In addition, the Church's teaching guides us in our beliefs and practices so that we can prepare adequately for eternity with God.

Unfortunately, however, people have lost their sense of sin because they have also lost their sense of the sacred. They do not believe that the Word became flesh (that is, that God became human in Jesus Christ) specifically because people of every time and place are sinners and need to be saved from the effects of their sins.

During these Advent weeks, we can prepare for Christ's arrival by imitating John the Baptist, a voice crying in the wilderness, and undergoing conversion from our sins. Advent is a particularly appropriate time to experience God's forgiveness by celebrating the sacrament of reconciliation, with genuine repentance and a determination to avoid the occasions of sin in the future. In this way we can truly look forward in hope to the Messiah's arrival both at Christmas and at the Last Judgement.

In adopting the spirit of the Advent season, we wait purposefully for Christ's arrival by preparing properly. John the Baptist is an ideal role model because of his fasting, penance and message of repentance. Reflecting on John, we pray that we too will become repentant for our sins so that we will be ready to meet the Lord whenever and however he comes.

For meditation
What must we do, then? (LUKE 3:10)

⊕
Fourth Sunday of Advent

GOSPEL READING: LUKE 1:39-45

REFLECTION

Almost since the beginning of Christianity, the Blessed Virgin Mary has been venerated as *Theotokos* (literally 'God-bearer'), recognising that she gave birth to the Son of God. Mary is frequently described as her Son's first disciple. Christian discipleship involves a commitment to Christ and she made an irrevocable commitment to him even before he was born. Her commitment was initially expressed at the Annunciation when, replying to the angel Gabriel's message, she said 'Yes' to God's request that she become the mother of his Son and that she cooperate with him by playing a central role in his plan for the salvation of humankind.

Like John the Baptist, Mary is one of the significant Advent people in the New Testament. How did she prepare for the arrival of the Messiah and in what way can she be a model of discipleship for us as we await Christ's coming into our lives?

Mary prepared for Christ's coming into her life very simply. She brought his presence which, paradoxically, was already in her own life – because he was a growing baby in her womb – into her cousin's life. She sensed Elizabeth's needs and she responded accordingly by reaching out and being present to her. Mary was thus a true disciple because she shared Christ's presence, thereby making a significant difference in Elizabeth's life. She literally took Christ to Elizabeth.

In one sense, there was nothing dramatic about Mary visiting her cousin who was in need. Her actions were quiet and uneventful. Yet, in another sense, Mary's unassuming response was precisely what was required from any true disciple. The most important and challenging task of all disciples is to share the presence of Christ, who is already in their lives, with everyone they meet.

This is done primarily by behaving decently and giving good example. As Christians, we are called to be different. We radiate Christ's light to those with whom we live and work and spend our leisure time. Our lifestyle stands out from those of the crowd. Where others cheat and steal, we are honest. Where they speak unkindly, we are charitable. We are faithful to Christ's teaching.

Hopefully, we have Christ's presence in our lives at all times. Just as he was present in Mary's womb, whenever we receive him in Holy Communion he is really and truly present in our lives. His presence lives in us. We easily forget that there are endless possibilities for sharing Christ's presence with other people.

If we are being unfaithful to Christ in any aspect of our lives, Advent is an ideal time for our conversion from sin to the life of grace. While there are many ways to prepare for Christmas, the simplest, but usually the most challenging, is to be conscious of Christ's abiding presence in our own lives and to be willing to share his presence with our families, colleagues and friends. To be aware of his presence in our lives and to bring his presence to others, we need, like Mary, to answer with an unqualified 'Yes' to his invitation to discipleship.

For meditation

Why should I be honoured with a visit from the mother of my Lord? (LUKE 1:43)

The Season of Christmas
⊕
The Nativity of Our Lord

GOSPEL READING (VIGIL MASS): MATTHEW 1:1-25
GOSPEL READING (MIDNIGHT MASS): LUKE 2:1-14
GOSPEL READING (DAWN MASS): LUKE 2:15-20
GOSPEL READING (MASS DURING THE DAY): JOHN 1:1-18

REFLECTION

Christmas has finally come. We rejoice that the Word has become flesh, that God the Son has become human while remaining divine. There is no more waiting because the Messiah has arrived and now is the time of liberation from our enslavement to sin. But this is not surprising since, in the Hebrew Scriptures (what Christians call the Old Testament), this arrival had been prophesied for many centuries before the birth of Christ.

The prophets taught that God would intervene dramatically in human history, redeeming his people by defeating the power of sin, thereby bringing an end to oppression and injustice (which are some of the consequences of sin), and by establishing freedom, peace and happiness. God would send the Saviour to rescue his people from their long-lasting trials and tribulations. As a result, the world and human life would never again be the same.

In Isaiah's words the prophecy was definite: 'For there is a child born for us, a son given to us and dominion is laid on his shoulders; and this is the name they give him: Wonder-Counsellor, Mighty-God, Eternal-Father, Prince-of-Peace. Wide is his dominion in a peace that has no end' (Isaiah 9:5-7). This particular prophecy is one of the most important messianic prophecies in the Hebrew Scriptures.

The prophecy was fulfilled at the Incarnation and the birth of Jesus. He is the 'Son of the Most High' (Luke 1:32) who was destined to be the Saviour of the world. He is the light that came into the world casting away the darkness of sin and cancelling human estrangement from God (see John 1:9).

We are the descendants, both historically and spiritually, of the many generations of people who 'walked in darkness' (Isaiah 9:1) for centuries as they waited and prepared for the Messiah's arrival. Sadly, we become lost in spiritual darkness whenever our lives are sinful. Our challenge at Christmas is to abandon sin and invite the light of Christ to shine in our lives.

When, with the light of God's grace, we overcome the darkness of sin, we are able to contribute to the ending of oppression and injustice in our world. That is what Jesus meant when, during his public ministry thirty years after his birth, he advised his disciples: 'Set your hearts on his kingdom first, and on his righteousness, and all these other things will be given you as well' (Matthew 6:33). Yet there is much disharmony and violence in our world. This is because countless numbers of people have not accepted Jesus as the Messiah and have not responded to his life-giving and redemptive message.

Christmas is a time for both giving and receiving gifts. The greatest gift that God gives us is sending his only Son among us to redeem us from the effects of sin. Christmas celebrates the reality that God is with us uniquely in and through Jesus Christ.

We are encouraged at Christmas to renew our hope in God because he has intervened spectacularly in history, particularly by becoming human, to save us from sin and death. Christmas is about life and light – the life offered us in Christ and his light which destroys the spiritual darkness of sin. We rejoice and are glad that he lives among us.

For meditation
Today in the town of David a saviour has been born to you; he is Christ the Lord. (LUKE 2:11)

⊕
The Holy Family of Jesus, Mary and Joseph

GOSPEL READING: LUKE 2:41-52

REFLECTION
The family is universally regarded as the nucleus or basic unit of society, whether secular or religious. It provides the foundation for the introduction of individual human beings to the wider community and society. Thus the family acts as a buffer or intermediary between individuals and the groups they join. This is why the family is important.

There are different understandings of what exactly the human family is and how it is structured. Traditionally, at least in Western civilisation, the family has been defined as a group of persons who are related by marriage or blood and which typically includes a mother, father and children. The group lives and works together for the common good of all the members and the relationships between members are central – the family offering security and support which nurtures the self-esteem and appreciates the dignity of each member.

Therefore, the family transmits a sense of belonging and its values to the members. The specifically Catholic understanding of the family maintains that the marriage between one woman and one man, which is at its core, is a sacrament which is celebrated and lived for life. Not surprisingly, then, marriage is regarded as being permanent and indissoluble.

However, there are many broken marriages in our society where one spouse and the children live apart from and are sometimes unsupported by the other spouse. Consequently, some children are reared in homes in which the father or the mother is absent or only occasionally present because of separation or divorce. Some family structures are made even more complicated by second or subsequent relationships which are now a common feature of society. The number of single-parent (that is, unmarried as distinct from widowed) families continues to increase. Sometimes children may not be aware of their father's identity. Obviously these family units are not within the parameters of the traditional family image.

A multitude of factors contributes to this changing situation. Life in modern society is particularly stressful. There is a general acknowledgement of society's increased demands on the family unit and the resulting increase in anxiety levels. Economic factors such as unemployment and poverty contribute immensely to the pressures on family stability, while emigration compels families to separate.

There are also contributing social factors. High levels of violence result in court convictions and prison sentences which threaten family structures and relationships. Domestic violence in its various forms – physical, mental and emotional – has devastating effects on most family members. Certain groups within society, such as the homeless and short-term fostered, rarely experience continuous family living. Others, perhaps through personal choice or because of their age or state of health or vocation, live alone or in community groups. In addition, religious faith is increasingly less important in the lives of many people.

There is an urgent need to renew family life. Research indicates that, when family members live together in harmony, the home provides the best environment for both social and faith development. That is why the family home may be accurately described as the domestic church. We read in Luke's Gospel that, in the family home in Nazareth, Jesus 'increased in wisdom, in stature, and in favour' (Luke 2:52) with God and other people. On the Feast of the Holy Family we pray and work for the renewal of family life in our Church and in society.

For meditation

Three days later, they found him in the Temple, sitting among the doctors, listening to them, and asking them questions; and all those who heard him were astounded at his intelligence and his replies.
(LUKE 2:46-47)

⊕

Solemnity of Mary, Mother of God

GOSPEL READING: LUKE 2:16-21

REFLECTION

At the beginning of the New Year many people make resolutions for the future and, although the passing of time proves that most people do not persevere, they intend to adhere faithfully and diligently to those resolutions. The New Year is usually a time of planning ahead, aspiring towards ideals, setting ambiguous targets and working to reach those ideals and achieve those targets.

Some people decide to devote more time to their spouses and children because they are conscious that, in the past, they have focused too much on work or other activities and neglected family life. Others resolve to work more efficiently so that they can honestly justify their earnings. Some students choose to study systematically and consistently, hoping that they will perform successfully in their examinations later in the year. Many people decide to become healthier by dieting and exercising, especially after their festive eating and drinking during the Christmas season.

But life is not as simple as making New Year resolutions and effortlessly keeping them. Experience teaches us that we are creatures of habit and that it is particularly difficult for most of us to remain disciplined enough to fulfil our New Year resolutions. In practice, we frequently abandon them soon afterwards, only to renew them again next year.

Christianity teaches us that human nature is flawed because of Original Sin and that, whenever we rely on ourselves alone, we are unable to sustain our efforts to change our attitudes and improve our behaviour. We constantly need God's help and blessing. Otherwise all our efforts are ultimately doomed to failure. Thus it is appropriate to ask God's blessing on the New Year and on everything we undertake in the future.

Invoking God's blessing and grace, which is a share in his divine life, on us and our activities acknowledges our dependence on God. It admits that we are people of faith. It also challenges us to be humble about our talents and achievements by reminding us that our happiness and well-being originate in God's infinite and unconditional love, which is the source of our life.

It is noteworthy that the Church begins the new civil year by celebrating the motherhood of Mary. The

Solemnity of Mary, Mother of God provides a possibility to renew our devotion to Mary, who is also Mother of the Church because she is our spiritual mother – and we are the Church. We begin the New Year by reflecting on Our Lady's humility and faith. She is a model for all Christians, and the beginning of the New Year is a good time to commit ourselves again to imitating her openness to God's will and her love for Christ and his Church.

What are our New Year resolutions? As we plan ahead and aspire towards ideals for the future, are we aware of the need for God in our lives? For example, will we start and finish each day with a prayer that asks for God's blessing? We begin another year by praying for God's blessing on our lives and on our work.

For meditation

As for Mary, she treasured all these things and pondered them in her heart. When the eighth day came and the child was to be circumcised, they gave him the name Jesus, the name the angel had given him before his conception. (LUKE 2:19, 21)

$$\oplus$$
Second Sunday after Christmas

GOSPEL READING: JOHN 1:1-18

REFLECTION

John's Gospel is quite different from those of Matthew, Mark and Luke. In contrast with their gospels, which begin by referring to this earthly world and the human Jesus, John's Gospel begins with eternity. Even the opening words indicate this clearly: 'In the beginning was the Word: the Word was with God and the Word was God' (John 1:1). The Word is inextricably linked with God for all eternity.

Thus John's Gospel begins with God and communicates the Christmas story from the perspective of God rather than from the standpoint of this world and human beings, which is how Matthew, Mark and Luke present their gospels. Therefore, John's Gospel may be described as more meditative and reflective than the synoptic gospels (the gospels of Matthew, Mark and Luke, which display much similarity in content and structure) because, being more spiritual, it invites us to become more reflective about the meaning of Christmas.

It is straightforward for us to relate to the very human image of the infant Jesus lying in the manger and wrapped in swaddling clothes. When we watch the figure of the infant Jesus being placed among the other figures in the crib during the Christmas Midnight Mass, we can easily imagine what it was like to be in the stable. We can readily identify with the human feelings and emotions of that moment.

However, it is much more difficult to relate to the more abstract concept of the Word becoming flesh. To do so requires serious reflection about what this means for our Christian lifestyle. Yet God desires that we would be reflective and prayerful people because he has given us the ability to think and meditate – like the people for whom John's Gospel was originally written.

The reality is that the infant Jesus lying in the manger is the Word of God who has become flesh. The birth of the infant Jesus in Bethlehem is the birth of the Word of God in the world. The infant Jesus is Emmanuel (God-with-us). He is the Word made flesh. This is the mystery of Christmas.

At Christmas Jesus is born anew in the heart of every committed Christian and, through his suffering humanity which he shares with each one of us, he gives us access to God's life and mystery. This is why we rejoice and give thanks.

We are called to be genuine Christmas people rejoicing that God, in the Word becoming flesh, has fulfilled his promise to send the Saviour into the world. In practice this means that we engage with the mystery of Christmas in a deeper way by turning away from sin and by recognising the presence of the new-born Christ in those around us. Perhaps we can pray best for this by modifying slightly a verse from St Paul's Letter to the Ephesians: may he enlighten the eyes of our minds so that we can see what hope his call holds for us, what rich glories he has promised the saints will inherit (see Ephesians 1:18).

For meditation
The Word was made flesh, he lived among us. (JOHN 1:14)

⊕
The Epiphany of the Lord

GOSPEL READING: MATTHEW 2:1-12

REFLECTION

For many Christians, the Feast of the Epiphany (which is also known as Little Christmas in Ireland) marks the end of the Christmas season. Yet the Epiphany is at the heart of the Christmas message. The word 'epiphany' means 'manifestation' or 'showing'. Fundamentally, the Christian vocation is to show Jesus and his glory to the world. The Epiphany acknowledges that Jesus Christ, the newborn baby, is the Saviour of all people.

During the Christmas season, we reflect on what it means to believe that the Word became flesh and lived among us. God has chosen to live among us, his people, in the person of Jesus Christ, our Lord and Saviour, who saves us from the justly deserved consequences of our sins.

This is why we celebrate Christmas. All other activities associated with Christmas – for example, the exchange of gifts, the holidays from school and work, the visits to family and friends – are secondary. The real wonder of Christmas is not just that God became human in and through his Son, Jesus Christ, but that Christ, through his Church, continues to be present in our world.

Christmas and the Epiphany challenge us to renew our appreciation of the commitment God has made to us by becoming human. In the person and life of Jesus Christ, the Word made flesh, God has demonstrated beyond all doubt how much he loves us and shares his life with us. God shares his life with us especially through the Church and the sacraments. In the person and life of Jesus Christ, God has embraced human nature completely and he has become one with it. This is the mystery of Christmas and it remains true for all time and for all God's people everywhere.

The Feast of the Epiphany invites us to consider once again the real meaning of Christmas and to respond accordingly. The wise men, in presenting Jesus with gifts of gold, frankincense and myrrh, acknowledged him as Saviour of all people. The feast invites us to ask: what gift can we present to Jesus that acknowledges him as our Saviour?

Surely the most appropriate gift is striving to live a life that imitates his teaching and example. Therefore, the Epiphany is an ideal time to reflect on the practice of our Christian faith so that, during the coming year, we will 'show' the world the glory of the Saviour who has redeemed us from sin and who gives us life through his Church and the celebration of the sacraments.

For meditation
We saw his star as it rose and have come to do the king homage. (MATTHEW 2:2)

⊕
The Baptism of the Lord

GOSPEL READING: LUKE 3:15-16, 21-22

REFLECTION

John the Baptist had already been baptising people before Jesus began his public ministry. John explained that his baptism was with water whereas Jesus' baptism would be with water, the Holy Spirit and fire. The difference between the two baptisms was significant. Nevertheless, Jesus chose to be baptised by John in the River Jordan.

Jesus' baptism was a defining moment in his life. It marked a departure from the years of relative anonymity (the hidden years, as they have sometimes been described) and the beginning of three years of public ministry. His baptism affected him greatly. He was revealed by the Father as being divine as well as human. He was commissioned to do the Father's will and he was assured that the Father's favour would be with him throughout his ministry.

During that ministry Jesus preached the Good News of salvation, worked many miracles and, ultimately, died on the cross to save us and all people from the consequences of sin. His ministry was effectively living the baptised life in union with God.

The sacrament of baptism is meant to be a defining moment in the lives of Christians. At baptism we are cleansed from sin through sharing in Christ's death and resurrection. We are chosen by God to be agents and instruments of the Good News.

Thus baptism marks the abandonment of sin and the acceptance of God's grace, which is given to us through Jesus Christ. We become brothers and sisters in Christ and our membership of the Church is initiated. Thereafter, our lives can never be the same again. There is a radical difference in our dignity and identity, provided that we assimilate the meaning of baptism in our lives.

The basic task for every Christian, then, is to live the baptised life. This means that we need to recognise that we have been chosen by God to share in Jesus' life and ministry. It involves welcoming the presence of the Holy Spirit into our lives who, working through the Church, influences our decisions. Living the baptised life requires us to imitate the teaching of Christ and his Church. We reject sin and we teach others by our inspired words and good example. Only then can God say to each one of us: 'You are my son/daughter; my beloved; my favour rests on you' (see Luke 3:22). Therefore, baptism offers us a new identity in Christ.

Unfortunately, however, the effects of baptism are often more symbolic than real. There are only minor changes in our lives and we continue to sin. We do not permit the grace of baptism to affect our attitudes and behaviour and there is little or no evidence of genuine conversion. If we are honest, we may admit that we might as well have never been baptised because baptism makes no difference to our lives.

The Feast of the Baptism of the Lord challenges us to reflect on our baptism and its significance in our lives. At a time when many people have abandoned God it is imperative that Christians are committed to living the baptised life. Unless we are faithful to our baptismal promises by rejecting evil and being obedient to Christ, we cannot claim to be authentic disciples and we cannot be genuine witnesses to the Good News.

For meditation

While Jesus after his own baptism was at prayer, heaven opened and the Holy Spirit descended on him in bodily shape, like a dove. And a voice came from heaven, 'You are my Son, the Beloved; my favour rests on you'. (LUKE 3:21-22)

The Season of Lent
⊕
First Sunday of Lent

GOSPEL READING: LUKE 4:1-13

REFLECTION

As the annual season of Lent begins, we are invited to renew our faith through prayer, acts of penance and charitable works. The greatest threat to our faith is surrendering to temptation, especially when, as Christians, we are obliged to avoid sin and choose what is good.

When confronted with persistent temptation in our lives, there are three possible approaches to dealing with it. The first is simply to yield to the temptation, as happened with Adam and Eve, often with sinful and tragic consequences.

Today we live in a very individualistic, consumerist society where immediate gratification is the norm. Therefore, many of us yield almost unthinkingly to the temptations that are presented so appealingly to us. For example, we 'flick' through various television channels trying to watch several programmes simultaneously. Such channel-hopping ensures that we do not satisfactorily see any of the programmes.

Partly as a result of being bombarded with sophisticated advertising and marketing strategies, we have developed a mentality that is governed primarily by the pleasure principle: everything must be convenient, pain-free and instant. Sunday trading, twenty-four hour services and on-line booking facilities have become features of contemporary society. Thus, when confronted by temptations that have sinful outcomes, we have limited experience of – and few skills in – dealing with them adequately. For instance, it is easier to be abrupt with people than patient, because we do not want to listen to them. Similarly, it is more convenient to tell a lie than speak the truth, to save embarrassment.

The second approach is to pray to God, asking him to remove the temptation. Asking God to remove temptation without acknowledging our own role in the situation is naïve because it is merely transferring complete responsibility to him. Surely, it is unfair when out drinking to 'have one more for the road' and then pray that we drive home safely. Many of us tend to leave it all to God hoping that, like a magician, he will take care of everything. But God does not work in this manner.

The third approach is best summarised by the cliché 'God helps those who help themselves'. This approach combines praying to God for help with taking responsibility through our own efforts. An example of this is the description of the temptations of Jesus in the wilderness. Jesus maximises his chances of fighting off temptation by fasting for forty days and, in doing so, turning completely towards God the Father and the influence of the Father's guidance and power.

Jesus' coping with temptation offers us not only hope but also a practical lesson in dealing successfully with temptation. If we are frequently in conflict with a colleague at work, it is not sufficient for us to pray that such conflict will stop. Rather, we are challenged to examine how, by modifying our behaviour, we can help to resolve the problem.

So, then, the message of the Good News is challenging and encouraging. It is challenging because resisting temptation requires effort and discipline, and sometimes pain. It is encouraging because such efforts, when combined with God's help and grace, which derive from prayer, bring about positive outcomes for us. Indeed, the Church recommends regular confession of our sins because celebrating the sacrament of reconciliation helps us to defeat temptation.

There are no shortcuts, no easy options, when dealing with temptation. God expects us to work with him instead of simply relying completely on him.

For meditation

Filled with the Holy Spirit, Jesus left the Jordan and was led by the Spirit through the wilderness, being tempted there by the devil for forty days. (LUKE 4:1-2)

⊕
Second Sunday of Lent

GOSPEL READING: LUKE 9:28-36

REFLECTION

During Lent, we are invited to be pilgrims on a journey with Jesus towards his suffering and death. Nevertheless, our pilgrimage does not stop with Jesus' death. Instead, it ends with the resurrection of Jesus from the dead and the glory he shares with us as our risen Lord and Saviour. The account of the Transfiguration of Jesus provides us with a glimpse of the glory that is his as the only Son of the Father.

But, for all the mystery that surrounds the Transfiguration of Christ, there is a simple yet very relevant message. The Transfiguration is a pointer towards Christ's future risen glory because he has been in union with the Father, aware that he must do the Father's will in all things in order to fulfil God's plan for salvation. The Father is proud of him and acknowledges this when he speaks in the voice coming from the cloud: 'This is my Son, the Chosen One. Listen to him' (Luke 9:35). It is in these words spoken by the Father that the real lesson is to be found.

We are also God's children. Just as the Father was able to describe Jesus as beloved and advise people to listen to him, so, too, the Father wishes to be able to say the same about each one of us, his sons and daughters – although we are God's children in a different way from Jesus Christ who is both divine and human.

Through our experience, God's voice is never heard speaking directly from the clouds. However, God's Holy Spirit, living in each one of us, desires to prompt us to recognise other people as God's children too. In doing so, the Spirit challenges us to listen to them and watch them, since they enjoy God's favour, so that we may learn more about God's glory from the evidence of it in their lives. The sure sign that the Holy Spirit is living in them is their faithfulness to the teaching of Christ and his Church.

Of course, the same principle applies to other people recognising us as God's children. But the prompting of the Holy Spirit will guide them to know us as God's children, of whom he is justifiably proud, only if, like Jesus, we are constantly open to the Father's influence in our lives. It is only when we radiate God's love through our adherence to Christ's teaching that we become recognisable as God's beloved children. If our lives are sinful then the Spirit will be unable to use us as examples for other people and God's glory will not be discernable in our lives.

The Transfiguration of Jesus teaches us about where our prayer and Lenten penance will lead us as we approach the feast of Easter. During the season of

Lent we get ready for Easter. By praying and doing acts of penance we prepare to be transformed by the risen life of Christ into radiant witnesses to God's love and glory. Thus we enter more fully into the mystery of the Transfiguration.

For meditation

As he prayed, the aspect of his face was changed and his clothing became brilliant as lightning.
(LUKE 9:29)

⊕
Third Sunday of Lent

GOSPEL READING: LUKE 13:1-9

REFLECTION

The call to repentance is at the heart of the Christian message and, because we are sinners, the season of Lent is the annual liturgical reminder about the need for ongoing repentance in our lives. Repentance requires humility and sincerity. It involves conversion (doing a complete U-turn), particularly away from sin and towards God's mercy as we struggle with the temptations of this world.

In his preaching, Jesus used the parable of the fig tree to alert his disciples to the need for repentance. Like his other parables, this parable is as relevant today as it was when Jesus told it. The barren fig tree is an image of the unproductive Christian life. Such a life occurs when we ignore the teaching of Christ and his Church and, ultimately, will result in disaster. Understandably, there is an urgency to become repentant for our sins and to undergo conversion. Otherwise, we cannot hope to gain eternal life with God. In the words of Jesus, we will 'perish' like some of 'the Galileans whose blood Pilate had mingled with that of their sacrifices' and 'those eighteen on whom the tower at Siloam fell' (Luke 13:1-4).

The parable has several lessons. Among them is the reality of God's infinite patience with us. God is just. But God is also merciful. His love for us is perfect and he gives us many chances to repent and change our lives – like the man caring for the vineyard who pleads for another chance for the fruitless fig tree. God never abandons us.

However, our chances are not endless because they cease when we die and, generally speaking, we do not know when death will happen. Our lives in this world are given to us by God so that, through them, we may prepare to be with him for eternity. Therefore, the Lenten message of repentance offers us an urgent 'Wake up!' call. Now is the time to examine our lives and begin to rid them of the various sinful attitudes and practices that prevent us from living in complete harmony with God.

There is no time like the present to do what is necessary to make the tree that is our life bear fruit. Instances of widespread sin in many of our lives include unjustified anger, bitterness and jealousy. Sometimes, too, we may be involved in gossip and slanderous conversation about other people. Or there may be physical violence and inappropriate sexual behaviour in our relationships.

Lent is effectively an annual retreat when we assess the quality of our relationships with God and with other people. As individuals, we learn from our mistakes in the past and we resolve not to repeat them again. As a Church, we learn from the lessons of history and we remind ourselves that the Church, too, is always in need of renewal and purification. We look forward in hope to a better life: the eternal life offered us by the risen Lord at Easter.

There is no time for complacency. Instead, there is a definite call to conversion and repentance so that we will be free to choose eternity with God whenever the moment of death comes. We cannot allow ourselves to be fooled into a false sense of security. Jesus teaches us that if we produce no fruits, we will be cut down. So, during Lent, we pray for the grace of true repentance. In addition, we celebrate the sacrament of reconciliation by going to confession and resolving not to sin again.

For meditation

Unless you repent you will all perish as they did.
(LUKE 13:5)

⊕
Fourth Sunday of Lent

GOSPEL READING: LUKE 15:1-3, 11-32

REFLECTION

The parable commonly referred to as the parable of the prodigal son is undoubtedly one of the most famous recorded in the New Testament. The term 'prodigal' means wastefully extravagant or lavish. Thus the parable could also be described as the parable of the wastefully extravagant son.

It would be foolish, however, to assume that our attention should be focused only on the prodigal son when we reflect on the parable. In addition to the younger son, the parable contains two other significant characters: the father and the elder son. Depending on the context in which the parable is read, it could also be described as the parable of the merciful father, the parable of the resentful son or, if comparing the two sons, the parable of the lost son and the dutiful son. No single title expresses satisfactorily the entire message of this parable and there are several lessons to be learnt.

The younger son was initially driven by greed and lust. He did not respect his father and his elder brother. He was ungrateful and impatient, unwilling to wait for his inheritance and anxious to be free from family work and ties. His behaviour was completely irresponsible. Like so many people today, his attitude was unashamedly: 'Eat, drink and be merry because tomorrow we die.' In this way he wasted his gifts and talents. He squandered the opportunities given to him. He sinned seriously.

The prodigal son was typical of people who are self-centred and indifferent towards the needs of other people. Eventually his crazy lifestyle ended and he paid a heavy price for his recklessness although, fortunately, his story did not end in total disaster. He repented before it was too late, having realised how wrong he had been, and, to his amazement, he rediscovered his father's unconditional love and forgiveness. In the parable, the most important detail about the younger son is not his selfishness but that he returned home repentant and experienced forgiveness.

The merciful father symbolises God's infinite mercy and tolerance towards us. The father was non-judgemental and forgiving. He was delighted that his younger son had undergone conversion from his sinful ·ways and had returned home. His forgiveness mirrors the forgiveness of God the Father. What a marvellous image of God for us. God does not quantify our sins. He readily forgives us and constantly draws us to himself.

Understandably, our sympathy might initially be with the elder brother. He was angry when he learned about the great welcome given by his father to the younger brother. He was self-righteous and full of self-pity. While he was unquestionably a dutiful son, he was also resentful. Like the younger son, he had rejected his father's love, although in a much less obvious way than his younger brother. The elder brother had sinned too.

There is a crucial lesson in this parable about God's love. Just as the father loved both sons, so God loves each one of us. The two sons could not earn their father's love and they did not deserve his love. Instead, they had to accept that it was freely given regardless of how they behaved. Such is God's love for us.

Finally, the father lost both sons – one to extravagance and the other to self-righteousness. He did everything to draw them back to himself. Therefore, the parable could also be described as the parable of the prodigal father in the sense of the father lavishing his love on both sons.

God is constantly inviting us to return to his loving care when we have sinned. We pray that, during Lent, we will become repentant for our sins and experience God's steadfast love again.

For meditation

Your brother here was dead and has come to life; he was lost and is found. (LUKE 15:32)

SEE THE TWENTY-FOURTH SUNDAY IN ORDINARY TIME FOR ANOTHER REFLECTION ON THE PARABLE OF THE PRODIGAL SON.

⊕

Fifth Sunday of Lent

GOSPEL READING: JOHN 8:1-11

REFLECTION

How easy it is to condemn other people. Many of us judge them automatically. Like the Pharisees and scribes in Jesus' time, we quickly focus on their mistakes and sins. We do not spare them embarrassment when we comment on their behaviour and rejoice at their humiliation, often having had their faults revealed publicly. Sometimes we are almost voyeuristic in our eagerness to discover how and when people have behaved indiscreetly and foolishly. It may be that they have been dishonest at work or unfaithful in their relationships.

Yet we apply different standards to ourselves. We are not so swift to criticise our own flaws and sins. In fact, we try to hide them in the hope that, if they are discovered, we will not be embarrassed and humiliated. While we are usually ready to disapprove of friends and colleagues, we have no desire to be condemned ourselves. Unfortunately, our double standards ensure that we do not treat other people as we would like them to treat us. We make excuses for our own unacceptable words and behaviour while, at the same time, demanding accountability from others for their transgressions.

Such hypocrisy contradicts the clear teaching of Jesus in the gospels. He did not condemn sinners, but he was uncompromising in his condemnation of their sins. He did not celebrate their downfall or delight in their shame. He rejoiced, instead, in their repentance because it enabled them to undergo conversion so that they could value and appreciate his forgiveness, which he shared freely with them. However, he always told them not to sin again.

Significantly, Jesus always practiced what he preached. He always loved the sinner while being repulsed by the sin and he instructed his disciples to do the same.

In the incident involving the woman caught committing adultery, Jesus exposed the hypocrisy of the Pharisees and the scribes by saying to them: 'If there is one of you who has not sinned, let him be the first to throw a stone at her' (John 8:7). Whereas they had initially been like vultures surrounding their prey, they were humbled by the simple words spoken by Jesus who highlighted the truth about them. The personal details of their sins might have differed from the woman's sins but, in reality, they were no different. They too were sinners in need of repentance. Importantly, Jesus offered great encouragement to the woman who, in more than one sense, was in a dangerous situation.

During Lent, we are invited to examine ourselves instead of focusing on other people. Before we begin to perceive their faults and sins, we are challenged to notice our own sins. Then, in a spirit of repentance, we can make the necessary amendments for them and seek God's forgiveness and the forgiveness of those we have hurt and offended. We will be so overjoyed at receiving God's forgiveness that we will no longer have the time or the desire to gloat over their sins. Instead we will have the option of encouraging them to repent so that they too may experience God's forgiveness and, as a result, sin no more.

For meditation

If there is one of you who has not sinned, let him be
the first to throw a stone at her. (JOHN 8:7)

⊕
Passion Sunday (Palm Sunday)

GOSPEL READING (The Procession): LUKE 19:28-40
GOSPEL READING (The Mass): LUKE 22:14–23:55

REFLECTION

The account of the Passion of Jesus Christ, which this
year is read from St Luke's Gospel, invites us to reflect
deeply on the price that Jesus paid for our redemption
from the consequences of our sins. Surely this fact
alone is sufficient meditation for an entire lifetime.

For example, there are disturbing details about the
betrayal, torture and crucifixion of Jesus. There are
descriptions of the shameful cruelty and inhumanity
of the crowd and soldiers. There are, too, several
depictions of the goodness of a few people who were
quite concerned about how Jesus was being treated.
And, of course, there are the words spoken by Jesus
that demonstrate clearly his mission and his total self-
giving, through his suffering and death, for the sins of
all people.

Perhaps, then, it may be helpful to focus on just
some of the passages from the Passion account and use
them in our prayer and reflection during Holy Week.
What are the particular phrases and passages that
strike us when we read the Passion? The following
inspire us to become more appreciative of God's love
for us in Christ and motivate us to repent for our sins:

- 'Then he took some bread, and when he had given thanks, broke it and gave it to them, saying, "This is my body which will be given for you; do this as a memorial of me". He did the same with the cup after supper, and said, "This cup is the new covenant in my blood which will be poured out for you".' (LUKE 22:19-20)

- 'Among pagans it is the kings who lord it over them, and those who have authority over them are given the title Benefactor. This must not happen with you. No; the greatest among you must behave as if he were the youngest, the leader as if he were the one who serves. For who is the greater: the one at table or the one who serves? The one at table, surely? Yet here I am among you as one who serves!' (LUKE 22:25-27)

- 'Jesus replied, "I tell you, Peter, by the time the cock crows today you will have denied three times that you know me".' (LUKE 22:34)

- 'Pray not to be put to the test.' (LUKE 22:40)

- 'Father, if you are willing, take this cup away from me. Nevertheless, let your will be done, not mine.' (LUKE 22:42)

- 'Pilate was anxious to set Jesus free and addressed them again, but they shouted back, "Crucify him! Crucify him!"' (LUKE 23:20-21)

- 'Daughters of Jerusalem do not weep for me; weep rather for yourselves and for your children.' (LUKE 23:28)

- 'Father, forgive them; they do not know what they are doing.' (LUKE 23:34)

- 'Indeed, I promise you, today you will be with me in paradise.' (LUKE 23:43)

- 'Jesus said, "Father, into your hands I commit my spirit". With these words he breathed his last.' (LUKE 23:46)

- 'When the centurion saw what had taken place, he gave praise to God and said, "This was a great and good man".' (LUKE 23:47)

Key questions for us during Holy Week are: how do we treat Jesus? Do we praise him when we are in the church and when we celebrate the sacraments and then quickly betray him as we return to sinful living? As we accompany him on his journey to Calvary, will we stay with him or will we – like many other people – abandon him?

For meditation
Jesus said, 'Father, forgive them; they do not know what they are doing'. (LUKE 23:34)

The Season of Easter

⊕

Easter Sunday

GOSPEL READING (Mass of Easter Night): LUKE 24:1-12
GOSPEL READING (Mass of the Day): JOHN 20:1-9

REFLECTION

For Jesus' disciples the days immediately after his resurrection from the dead were very cherished days. At first they did not recognise him so easily because there seemed to be some difference in his physical appearance. Yet he spoke to them, walked among them and ate with them just as he had done before his crucifixion and death a few days earlier.

However, the significance of the days after the resurrection for his disciples was that they were slowly, but surely, able to recognise and acknowledge him for who he really is: the Son of God, the Saviour of the world, the one who had begun to have such an impact and good influence on each of their lives. Their despair and hopelessness were dispelled by new hope and impressive conviction. Gradually, they began to understand that death is never the end but, rather, the beginning. Therefore, the resurrection of Jesus from the dead had definite implications for his disciples.

What exactly were those implications? After the resurrection, the disciples began to realise that everything Jesus had said and done – which before his death had seemed incredible – was indeed true. He had spoken the truth and lived according to the truth. His resurrection was proof, if ever proof was needed. Consequently, Jesus' rising from the dead changed everything utterly for them. Now that he had risen he was present to them again in a very real and intimate way. His risen presence offered them reassurance and the possibility of renewing their commitment to him and his teaching.

The days after the first Easter gave Jesus' disciples the opportunity to appreciate and marvel at his risen presence in their lives. They were able to respond with renewed dedication and hope-filled hearts. They could reassess their attitudes and lifestyle and begin to put into practice Jesus' teaching and example of selflessness, compassion and, most importantly, forgiveness. In this way, they were to become great witnesses to the entire world for the risen Lord Jesus.

Focusing instead on ourselves, we are also disciples of Jesus, and Easter Sunday and the following days are very cherished days for us too. The reality is that we are always living in the days after the Resurrection. Like the first disciples, the resurrection of Jesus from the dead has implications for us. We are ready to meet the risen Jesus whenever he enters our lives. His risen presence is always available to us, especially in word and sacrament, if only we welcome him with open and renewed hearts. So as we meet other people we have an occasion to respond in love to our risen Lord. As genuine disciples of Christ, we need to bring out what is best in ourselves by helping to bring out what is best in others. This is the only way that what happened at Easter will become truly meaningful in our lives.

During the days after Easter our faith challenges us to ask what difference does the resurrection of Jesus make in our lives. The Easter liturgical celebrations invite us to think about and reflect seriously on the implications of the resurrection for our faith and lifestyle. We realise that death is never the end and that, with the risen Christ, there is indeed life after death. If we believe this and live accordingly, then, like the first disciples, we will be witnesses to the entire world for the risen Lord Jesus. Alleluia! Alleluia!

For meditation

Why look among the dead for someone who is alive?
(LUKE 24:5)

⊕
Second Sunday of Easter

GOSPEL READING: JOHN 20:19-31

REFLECTION

Reflecting on God's forgiveness of our sins, we soon appreciate that the fundamental truth about all of us is that God loves us and accepts us for who we are. The most effective way to realise this truth in our lives is to receive God's forgiveness graciously and permit it to radiate from our lives and permeate all our relationships. This empowers us to let go of hurt and resentment so that integrity and honesty may be restored where necessary.

The English word 'forgive' derives from an older English phrase 'forth give'. Thus forgiveness is about forth-giving. In other words, to forgive someone is to give forth of myself to that person, although he or she has offended me and hurt me. Forgiveness means continuing to relate to that person as if the hurt or offence had never occurred. It implies allowing that person into my 'space' again without constructing barriers or imposing conditions. Basically, then, forgiveness involves letting go and giving that person another chance. This is precisely what happens every time God forgives (or gives forth of himself). God does not place any barriers or enforce any conditions that prevent us from revisiting his 'space'.

However, giving forth of ourselves to somebody who has mistreated us involves taking a risk. It requires that we trust the person not to act in the same hurtful and offensive manner as before. There are times when we are challenged to work at forgiving unconditionally, especially when some people do not understand that they have caused hurt and damage. Elsewhere in the gospels Jesus prays: 'Father, forgive them; they do not know what they are doing' (Luke 23:34).

It is not surprising that we might be reluctant to be hurt again by offering an additional opportunity for friendship and respect. Yet, that is what Jesus calls us to do. Following Jesus is risky. The practice of forgiveness is hazardous. Giving forth of ourselves is perilous. In fact, in taking this risk we can only hope that there is some indication that the person values the opportunity for renewal that is being offered. This is especially true when God, working through the ordained priest, forgives our sins in the sacrament of reconciliation.

The absence of forgiveness is like a spiritual cancer that, unless challenged, destroys the fabric of our lives. Very often, we ourselves are the first victims of our lack of forgiveness. Some of us live with doubts and regrets, and regrets cause us to regress. We refuse to forgive ourselves, or to accept that others have forgiven us, and we do not let go of the past.

More often, however, we may deny forgiveness to people who have offended us. This can apply to family members, neighbours, friends and colleagues at work or in school. We harbour bad feelings towards them. We wish them bad luck. We despise their happiness and we resent their good fortune. We hold hatred in our hearts towards them and we demand revenge. We avoid people with whom we have rowed and argued.

We forget – or conveniently choose to deny – that God has forgiven us.

Each one of us needs to imitate God's example, particularly if we claim to be followers of Jesus Christ. Even at the heart of the model for prayer that Jesus taught his disciples is the crucial phrase: 'And forgive us our debts, as we have forgiven those who are in debt to us' (Matthew 6:12). Forgiveness is essential to Christianity. Today we welcome God's forgiveness in our lives.

For meditation

Jesus came in and stood among them.
'Peace be with you,' he said. (JOHN 20:26)

⊕
Third Sunday of Easter

GOSPEL READING: JOHN 21:1-19

REFLECTION

Jesus appeared to his disciples many times after his resurrection from the dead. On those occasions, they did not always recognise him initially, but when he spoke to them they were able to identify him as 'the Lord' (John 21:7). Among the locations where he appeared to them were the garden, the upper room, the road to Emmaus, the hillside and the lakeshore where they had gone fishing.

Jesus' appearance on the lakeshore was particularly important because he tested Peter's faith by asking him three times: 'Do you love me?' (John 21:15). This persistent questioning by Jesus paralleled the three times Peter had denied Jesus in the courtyard of the High Priest's house on the night before Jesus was crucified.

When Peter answered 'Yes' each time to Jesus' question, he was effectively undoing the damage done to his relationship with Jesus by the earlier denials.

Peter had not been a loyal friend to Jesus when Jesus needed him. He revoked his commitment to Jesus and deserted him, choosing instead the cowardly option of denial so that he could not be implicated as one of Jesus' followers. On the lakeside, after the resurrection, Jesus offered Peter a second chance. Jesus was not interested in the past because he had already forgiven Peter. All that mattered was the sincerity of Peter's love. Peter's threefold profession of love was a sign of the new quality of his faith and a renewal of his commitment to Jesus.

Significantly, on the basis of Peter's profession of love, Jesus invited Peter to follow him again and he commissioned Peter to feed and care for his flock. Peter would lead the disciples and the early Church with the assurance of Jesus' constant presence and guidance. Central to Peter's mission (and, indeed, the mission of his successors, the popes) was the task of teaching the truths that are essential for salvation.

Eastertide offers us a chance to prove our love for Jesus by renewing our commitment to him and his teaching. Genuine love involves much more than romance and sentimentality. In addition, it often entails sacrifice and suffering. It demands faithfulness to God, our friends and our responsibilities. Our love for other people flows from our love for God. Love requires dedication to loved ones in every situation and all circumstances. This was exactly the kind of love that Jesus required from Peter. It is the kind of love that Jesus requires from us.

So often we fail to recognise the presence of the risen Jesus in our lives and in our world. Surely this is due to our lack of faith and our sinfulness. Before Jesus appointed Peter to a pivotal role within the Church, he tested Peter's faith. Our ambition as Christians must be to aspire to true faith and real love of God, especially in an increasingly amoral and secular world. Like Peter, we must be able, truthfully, to say: 'Lord, you know everything; you know I love you' (John 21:17).

For meditation
Jesus then stepped forward, took the bread and gave it to them, and the same with the fish. (JOHN 21:13)

⊕
Fourth Sunday of Easter

GOSPEL READING: JOHN 10:27-30

REFLECTION

Easter celebrates the joy and glory of the risen Lord Jesus. It acknowledges that he is indeed the Good Shepherd who lays down his life for his sheep. He is completely faithful to his heavenly Father's will. Yet submitting to it had very serious implications for him.

Jesus loved sinners so much that he suffered and died for them. We need to realise that we are among those sinners and that we contributed to Jesus' suffering. But, as we know, Jesus' shepherding role did not end with his death on the cross. God raised him from the dead and, as a result, he freely shares his risen life with all those who, through baptism, have become brothers and sisters. Living the baptised life requires that we imitate Jesus' example by obeying the Father's will.

Jesus was a marvellous communicator. He used the image of the shepherd when teaching about the nature of God because he knew that his audiences understood the work of a shepherd and that they could easily distinguish between good and bad shepherds. Good shepherds ensured that their sheep were safely locked in pens at night. They double-checked that no other animals had slipped in, animals that might harm the unsuspecting sheep.

Vigilance is the watchword of good shepherds and that is what Jesus asks us to be vigilant in our fight against temptation and sin, aware that we need the Good Shepherd's help to remain safe spiritually. Thus the challenge today is precisely the same as that facing the first century disciples of Jesus: to be ready to suffer and, if necessary, to die for him.

Being followers of Jesus demands that we are willing to be inconvenienced and, when necessary, to be prepared to suffer in defending our faith. This involves struggling to perfect our fallen human nature by, for example, putting the needs of other people first, rather than being self-centred and selfish. This is what Jesus demonstrated by his preaching and lifestyle.

The reason why Jesus was able to behave so decently and honourably towards those who treated him badly was because he was always in perfect union with God his heavenly Father who loved him and supported him. Jesus knew that, regardless of the circumstances in which he found himself, he was never alone. God never deserted him. This knowledge gave him great consolation and encouragement.

In imitating Jesus' example, we are challenged by the Good News to imitate his behaviour, whatever the circumstances. We recognise and look to him as the Good Shepherd who never leaves us untended.

For meditation

The sheep that belong to me listen to my voice; I know them and they follow me. I give them eternal life; they will never be lost and no one will ever steal them from me. (JOHN 10:27-28)

⊕
Fifth Sunday of Easter

GOSPEL READING: JOHN 13:31-35

REFLECTION

Love is the main characteristic of Christianity because Jesus' teaching can be summarised in his great commandment: 'Love one another; just as I have loved you, you also must love one another' (John 13:34). Also, Jesus taught that it is by our love for one another that people will know that we are his disciples. In addition to loving God through our personal relationship with Jesus, we express our love for God through our love for other people. For this reason, we cannot claim to love God if we do not love them.

There is a significant difference between liking someone and dutifully loving someone in the Christian sense of loving. Many people assume that the two words, 'like' and 'love', have the same meaning. Such confusion makes it difficult to appreciate Jesus' commandment to love other people. Unfortunately, reality suggests that there are usually at least some people in all our lives that we do not particularly like.

Loving, in the Christian context, is not a more intense form of liking. To like people means that we experience them as being agreeable or pleasant. In contrast, to love people means that, regardless of whether or not we consider them agreeable or likeable, we respect them. We are always patient with them and kind towards them. To love people means that we are neither rude to them nor arrogant towards them. It means that we never become irritable and resentful towards them.

True love requires us to care about others, always putting them first. We cannot truly love God if we do not love them. The basic challenge of the Good News is to love all people, including those we dislike.

This does not just mean 'being nice' in our relationships. Jesus was known for his 'hard sayings' that challenged his listeners to change their lifestyles. We are obliged to be faithful to the truth and to speak the truth with respect and compassion. Thus loving others means having an active concern for their welfare – especially their spiritual welfare. No wonder, then, that Christianity is demanding. Actually it is impossible if we rely only on ourselves. We require God's grace and strength if we are to succeed.

The message is clear: no matter how disagreeable or unsuitable we find other people, we are challenged by Jesus' great commandment to love those people always. For Christians, as difficult as it may be, it is possible to love people without necessarily liking them. Loving people is not an optional extra for us. It is a serious obligation.

The basis for Christian love is Jesus' self-giving which was so perfect that he offered his life on the cross to undo the effects of our sins. His commandment to love one another just as he has loved us implies that we too will be expected to make sacrifices as we put the needs of others before our own needs. That demands considerable effort on our part and, as we know, is not always easily achieved.

The fundamental question is: how genuine is our love? Although we may not like all the people in our lives, Jesus has made love the distinguishing mark of his Church. As Christians, then, we are obliged to love one another, and it is this mutual love that becomes the sign to the world that we are Jesus' disciples.

For meditation
I give you a new commandment: love one another.
(JOHN 13:34)

⊕

Sixth Sunday of Easter

GOSPEL READING: JOHN 14:23-29

REFLECTION

It is often said that God never closes one door without opening another. This is especially relevant when Jesus tells his disciples that he is about to leave them. It seems that the end is near, that God is closing the door which has opened his love to the world.

However, this suggestion is not true because, while Jesus is leaving, another door is being opened to his disciples. Jesus promises them the constant presence of the Advocate, the Holy Spirit, who will inspire and motivate them. This promise comforts them as they begin to realise that Jesus will no longer be with them. The Holy Spirit will remind them about all that Jesus has taught them during his time with them.

Just as any good father, although separated from his children, is always with them in mind and in spirit, God is forever with us, his people. The Holy Spirit, the Advocate, who is the Third Person of the Blessed Trinity, encourages Jesus' disciples and rekindles his teaching and example in them. The presence of the Holy Spirit empowers the disciples to persevere in life's dilemmas and conflicts without losing faith.

We speak of the Holy Spirit empowering Jesus' disciples. But we too are Jesus' disciples and his message is for us. God has given each one of us the gift of free will. Free will is about choice. It requires that we make decisions. Here God opens a door. We may choose to remain outside or to accept the invitation into a relationship with the Holy Spirit, the Advocate. In this relationship, the Holy Spirit guides our lives by influencing our choices and enlightening our decisions. The Spirit assists us to love Jesus by keeping his word. The Spirit also teaches us to recognise the difference between good and bad, between right and wrong.

Thus the Holy Spirit makes a major difference in our lives if we welcome his presence because he helps us to realise that God lives within us. We constantly need to be aware of God's presence. When we understand that God lives in us and when we sense God's presence, then we are at peace. The Spirit gives us peace, peace that the world cannot give. Furthermore, we are asked to share this peace with other people. In doing so, we help to bring them closer to God.

So, then, while Jesus prepares to leave his disciples, God opens another door. As disciples of Jesus we are challenged to dedicate our lives to him, confident that the Holy Spirit will teach us everything through the Church if we are open and willing. Jesus reminds us that we must not let our hearts be troubled or afraid. He never leaves us unaccompanied and unaided.

The Holy Spirit will be with us until the end of time. The question for us is: will we welcome and accept the gift of the Holy Spirit every day? We step forward together in faith, in that knowledge that the Spirit transforms us into the living people of the Resurrection if we are faithful to the teaching of Christ and his Church. Jesus' historical presence in the world may be ending, but God never closes one door without opening another.

For meditation

The Advocate, the Holy Spirit, whom the Father will send in my name, will teach you everything and will remind you of all I have said to you. (JOHN 14:26)

⊕
The Ascension of the Lord

GOSPEL READING: LUKE 24:46-53

REFLECTION

In order to appreciate the Church's nature (that is, what the Church actually is) and its role in the world, we need to understand as fully as possible the Church's mission. This is because, essentially, the Church's nature is the Church's mission. And as members of the Church, we are obliged to participate in its mission.

The Church's mission is best summarised in the mandate given by Jesus to his disciples before he ascended to heaven, having accomplished what the Father had sent him to do. He had been sent into the world to save God's people from the devastation of sin so that they might have life to the full. Jesus had taught that he is the Way, the Truth and the Life.

At the Ascension, before moving beyond their sight, Jesus told his disciples to continue his saving activity. They were to be his witnesses. They were to make disciples of all the nations by going out to the whole world. They were effectively commissioned to lead people to conversion by proclaiming the Good News to everyone, thus bringing them to salvation. They were to teach those who were baptised to observe all that Jesus had taught during his earthly ministry.

So the Ascension was not the conclusion of Christ's redemptive work. Rather, it marked the handing over of his mission to his disciples and, in turn, to their disciples. It was the beginning of their response in faith to all that he had done for them. He was making each of them 'another Christ' who would assume some responsibility for continuing Christ's saving work among the peoples of the world.

Thus his physical departure had implications for his disciples − including us. This is the basis of the Church. This is why the Church's mission and the Church's nature are identical. Both are of divine origin.

Although Jesus has ascended to the Father, he continues to be present to us in many ways. He is present in the word of God as it is proclaimed in truth and faithfulness, especially when we gather to celebrate the sacred liturgy. He is present in a unique way in the Church's sacraments when they are celebrated, and particularly by his real and abiding presence in the Eucharist. He is present in each one of us, his brothers and sisters through baptism, as we live in accordance with his teaching and example. While he is no longer present in a human body, he is present in many other ways. The Holy Spirit is also with us.

The Feast of the Ascension is a call to renew our participation in the Church's mission. We help to make disciples by our words and good example. When we are committed to the Church and its teaching, we help those who are preparing for baptism. We teach other people about the eternal life that is offered to them whenever we speak about our faith and its relevance to our lives. This is how we participate in the Church's mission and begin to understand more fully its nature.

On the Feast of the Ascension we focus our minds and hearts not so much on Jesus' departure from this world but rather on his continued presence among us, albeit in different ways. While his earthly mission concludes with the Ascension, his mission of salvation continues in the Church. We, together, are the Church. We are the Body of Christ which is a sign of God's loving presence to the entire world. We are reminded to assume the responsibility that comes with baptism as we renew our commitment to being the Church and to loving the Church.

For meditation

As he blessed them, he withdrew from them and was carried up to heaven. (LUKE 24:51)

⊕
Seventh Sunday of Easter

GOSPEL READING: JOHN 17:20-26

REFLECTION

While preparing for Pentecost, we reflect on the final part of the priestly prayer of Jesus. In that prayer, he hoped that his disciples would believe that he loved them as much as the Father loved him. Only true love can unite us in the Church. That is why we are challenged to be genuine in professing our love for others.

Regrettably, we are not always genuine when telling other people that we love them. Sometimes, when they attempt to correct us, we charm them by saying 'I love you'. Similarly, we disarm their efforts to offer advice that we do not want. But there is no change in our attitudes and behaviour that would indicate our sincerity. Our tactic is simply one of avoiding embarrassment.

The reality is that many of us are careless about saying 'I love you'. Our carelessness is unintended but that is precisely the problem. We do not appreciate the true meaning of love. The same applies to our relationship with God.

Jesus taught his disciples that the greatest and the first commandment is to love God and that the second commandment is to love our neighbour as ourselves. Yet many of us are not genuine when we say to God and other people: 'I love you.'

True love requires us to care about others, putting them first. Elsewhere in the New Testament, we read that love is patient and kind. It is never jealous, boastful or conceited. Love is never rude or selfish. It does not take offence and is not resentful. It delights in the truth and is always ready to excuse and trust (see 1 Corinthians 13).

We cannot truly love God if we do not genuinely love other people. While we can love our neighbour without loving God, we cannot love God without loving our neighbour. Do we really love God and do we love the Church, which is meant to be a loving community? The proof of our love is to be found in whether or not we keep the commandments. Being faithful to the commandments teaches us the real meaning of love.

The challenge of the Good News is both simple and difficult. We relate to God directly, especially when we celebrate the sacraments, but God's presence is also to be found in the people we meet every day: our families at home, our friends in school and our colleagues at work. Jesus taught that when we are charitable to those in need, we are also being charitable to him. We are commanded to love others and treat them as we would treat Christ himself.

Let us think carefully before saying 'I love you' to God or someone else. We need to ask ourselves: do we really mean what we are about to say? If we do not, then let us not say it. God's commandment to love invites us to appreciate the wonder of God's life shared freely with us and experienced through other people who, like us, are made in God's image and likeness.

For meditation
May they be so completely one that the world will realise that it was you who sent me and that I have loved them as much as you loved me. (JOHN 17:23)

⊕
Pentecost Sunday

GOSPEL READING (MASS DURING THE DAY): JOHN 14:15-16, 23-26

REFLECTION

Pentecost was indeed a strange day for the apostles. Ten days previously, Jesus had ascended to heaven. He had promised to send the Advocate, the Holy Spirit, who would teach them, guide them and maintain harmony and unity among them. On Pentecost, something very strange happened. While they were together, Jesus' promise was fulfilled as they received the outpouring of the Holy Spirit.

Pentecost was not the first occasion on which the apostles received the Holy Spirit. However, unlike previous occasions, at Pentecost they were 'filled' with the Holy Spirit who lavished various gifts on them. The significance of the Holy Spirit descending on them was that their lives were transformed so that they could become powerful and courageous witnesses for Christ.

Consequently, everything changed for the apostles. They were blessed with the indwelling of the Holy Spirit. Any one of them could have rejected the Spirit because the Spirit never forces himself or his gifts on anyone. But they freely chose to accept the Spirit and his gifts in their lives. The gifts included wisdom, understanding, right judgement, courage, knowledge, reverence, and wonder and awe in God's presence.

Thus from being an almost insignificant community, they were transformed into the Church with a definite mission and a mandate to travel to the ends of the earth sharing with other people their knowledge and experiences of Christ. They became fearless and uncompromising preachers of the Good News. They realised that they could no longer be hesitant about proclaiming Christ's teaching. Their lives would never again be the same.

The apostles used the gifts of the Holy Spirit as they encouraged people to turn away from sin and as they transformed the world so that the kingdom of God could emerge in people's lives. Although in earlier days they had deserted Jesus, most of them were eventually martyred because of their later faithfulness to his teaching. Pentecost was certainly a turning point in their lives.

Applying this truth to ourselves, the sacrament of confirmation is our personal Pentecost event. It is the great sacrament of transformation. In confirmation we are 'filled' with the Holy Spirit and we receive the gifts of the Holy Spirit. Our lives are transformed so that, like the apostles, we can be courageous witnesses for

Christ. But also like them, we must choose daily to welcome and accept the Spirit.

When we are responsive to the Holy Spirit in our lives, we joyfully proclaim the truth of God's word in every situation whatever the consequences. We remain committed to the Church as the guardian and teacher of the faith. We turn away from sin. By doing so, we begin to transform the world so that God's presence is always glorified and many of the effects of the gifts of the Holy Spirit (what we call the fruits of the Holy Spirit) become evident in our lives. Among these effects are charity, joy, peace, patience, kindness, goodness, generosity, gentleness, faithfulness, modesty, self-control and chastity.

Pentecost emphasises the continuous outpouring of the Holy Spirit on the Church and the Church's worldwide mission. It also reminds us about the sacrament of confirmation and the personal transformation that is possible in our lives if we are open to the promptings and guidance of the Spirit.

We welcome the outpouring of the Holy Spirit on our Church and on our world. We renew our commitment to the Good News of Christ and, always prompted by the Holy Spirit, we confess that Jesus is Lord.

For meditation

The Advocate, the Holy Spirit, whom the Father will send in my name, will teach you everything and will remind you of all I have said to you. (JOHN 14:26)

⊕ SOME FEASTS OF THE LORD IN ORDINARY TIME

⊕
The Most Holy Trinity

Gospel reading: John 16:12-15

Reflection

Some people mistakenly assume that the central doctrine (or teaching) of the Christian faith is that Jesus Christ is both divine and human. Others claim that Jesus' resurrection from the dead is the central doctrine. However, while these beliefs are fundamental to Christianity, neither of them is its pivotal doctrine. The core teaching of the Christian faith is the doctrine of the Trinity which is the most overwhelming Christian mystery. The doctrine of the Trinity is Christianity's answer to the question: who is God?

Essentially, the doctrine of the Trinity teaches us that there are Three Persons in One God. God is Father and Son and Holy Spirit. Yet the Father is not the Son or the Holy Spirit, the Son is not the Father or the Holy Spirit, and the Holy Spirit is not the Father or the Son. We may well ask: how can there be Three Persons in One God? In human thinking, 'three persons' means 'three individuals'. So how can God be different? One answer is that God is beyond human reason. God is Mystery.

Because the Trinity is Mystery, it has never been possible for the Church to explain it – although, throughout history, the Church has stated the doctrine in its various creeds. Nevertheless, there is much evidence for the Trinity in God's revelation or self-communication.

While there is no explicit doctrine of the Trinity in the Bible, the doctrine is prefigured in the Old Testament when God visits Abraham (see Genesis 18:1-15). But the most significant indications that there are Three Persons in One God is in the New Testament where Jesus stresses the Father's unconditional love, his own equality with the Father, and the outpouring of the Holy Spirit to unite and guide his disciples.

Jesus is the fullness of God's revelation, especially when he teaches that God loved the world so much that he sent his only Son to save the world from the consequences of sin. He commissioned his disciples to share the truth they had been taught by him, and that they had begun to appreciate, by baptising and teaching in the name of the Father and of the Son and of the Holy Spirit.

Through our experiences we relate to God in different ways. God is our Creator (the Father). But God is also our Redeemer (the Son) and our Sanctifier (the Holy Spirit). As Father and Son and Holy Spirit, God's love is real. The basic truth about God is that God is love and, in particular, that God is love in Jesus Christ. The relationship between the Son and the Father and the Holy Spirit is a perfect relationship based on equality and mutual love.

We are made in God's image and likeness. We are challenged to reflect the perfect love that is found in

God. This means that we are called to be perfect just as our heavenly Father is perfect. We are asked to be prepared to lay down our lives for our neighbour. We are invited to work at sustaining peace and unity among all God's people. In summary, we are asked to believe in the God of Jesus Christ: God who is Father and Son and Holy Spirit.

So the questions we need to ask on this feast are: do we believe in the God of Jesus Christ? How God-like are we in our daily lives? Is our love for God and other people perfect, so that our Christian faith is a genuinely Trinitarian faith? Are we living in the Mystery of the Most Holy Trinity?

For meditation

Everything the Father has is mine; that is why I said: All he [the Spirit] tells you will be taken from what is mine. (JOHN 16:15)

⊕
The Body and Blood of Christ

GOSPEL READING: LUKE 9:11-17

REFLECTION

In the story of the five loaves and the two fish, we learn that Jesus fed the hungry crowd by multiplying five barley loaves and two fish. He did this because he was concerned for the people who had stayed with him, listening to him and watching him cure the sick. In a sense, he was acknowledging their commitment to spending time with him.

Initially, Jesus tested his disciples by asking them where they might get something for the hungry crowd to eat. They had no practical answer to his question, however, and they felt quite powerless. Then Jesus began to teach them by example. This is significant because Jesus always practiced what he preached. He never asked other people to do what he was unwilling to do himself. He satisfied the crowd's physical hunger and, in doing so, he enhanced the authority of what he had already said to them and of what he had already done when he cured the sick.

Interestingly, the multiplication of the loaves and fish is Jesus' only public miracle that is recorded in each of the four gospels, thus stressing its importance for the Christian community. The love and generosity of Jesus in tending to the needs of the hungry crowd offer us an insight into his own total self-giving for others at the Last Supper and in his suffering and death.

Jesus' miracle of the five loaves and the two fish, which responded to the physical hunger of the crowd, foreshadowed his miracle at the Last Supper when he shared himself in the Eucharist, the Bread of Life, with his disciples, thereby satisfying their spiritual hunger. It is surely noteworthy that Jesus had enough food for everybody, and then some remaining.

The lesson of the miracle of the loaves and fish is obvious: Jesus, who responded to and reached out to people in their need, wants his disciples to do the same. The question for all of us is: do we share ourselves, our gifts and our time with other people when they are needy? In other words, what are we prepared to do to help people avoid sin and save their souls? We are challenged to appreciate one another just as Jesus appreciated the crowd that had gathered to listen to him.

It can be particularly difficult to put other people's needs before our own. However, that is what we are called to do as Christian disciples. In the miracle of the five loaves and the two fish, Jesus relied on his Father's help as he responded to a crisis. Likewise, we who are Jesus' disciples need to rely on his help as we respond to crises and needs around us. Jesus taught by example when he fed the hungry crowd. He instructed his disciples to do the same.

Can we once again begin to appreciate our total dependence on God's endless love and mercy in Jesus Christ? In the same spirit, can we stop asking other people to do what we are unwilling to do ourselves? Let us, therefore, give generously and receive graciously, always imitating the generosity of our Lord and Saviour Jesus Christ who gives us the gift of himself in the Eucharist.

For meditation
They all ate as much as they wanted. (LUKE 9:17)

SUNDAYS IN ⊕
ORDINARY TIME

⊕
Second Sunday in Ordinary Time

GOSPEL READING: JOHN 2:1-11

REFLECTION

There are at least three lessons to be learned from the story of the wedding feast at Cana in Galilee. Firstly, there is the changing of the water into wine indicating that Jesus is divine as well as human. Secondly, there is the presence of Jesus at the wedding celebration and his willingness to help the newly married couple. Thirdly, there are the words of Mary, the mother of Jesus, who tells the servants: 'Do whatever he [Jesus] tells you' (John 2:5).

The changing of the water into wine was indeed a miracle. Interestingly, the writer of the Fourth Gospel describes Jesus' action as a 'sign' rather than as a 'miracle' and he writes that the changing of the water into wine was the 'first of the signs given by Jesus' (John 2:11). The Cana story reveals that Jesus is divine. No mere human being could perform miracles.

Fundamentally, all the miracles worked by Jesus during his public ministry were signs pointing to his true identity. Thus the miracles were much more than acts of kindness and compassion. They were effective signs that revealed the truth about him and why he had come into this world. Jesus came to show all people the Father's endless love and to redeem them from their captivity to sin. The signs of power and healing associated with his ministry were glimpses of eternity. They invited people to consider repentance and conversion so that they could strive for a share in eternal life.

There is also the presence of Jesus at the wedding and his willingness to assist the newly married couple who could easily have been embarrassed after there was no more wine available for the guests. He did not abandon them in their hour of need and he made a significant difference to their celebration.

Similarly Jesus is present in all our lives and relationships. He is the silent partner at every wedding and the unseen guest in every home. He is ready to help us in all our difficulties. However, we need to acknowledge his presence and be open to his influence in our various activities, trusting him completely so that he can lead us and guide us.

Finally, there are few but wise words spoken by Mary: 'Do whatever he tells you' (John 2:5). Mary is a woman who speaks few words in the gospels. Yet she could not have spoken more relevant and challenging words to the servants. Her advice is as good nowadays as it was at the wedding in Cana. If the servants had not heeded her advice, Jesus would not have given his first sign.

Mary, who is our mother and the Mother of the Church, always offers the same advice to us. She encourages us to do whatever Jesus tells us. This means that we are invited to listen attentively to the teaching of Jesus and his Church and to put it into practice in our daily lives. That is a demanding task. It is often easier and more tempting to ignore his teaching. It is far more difficult to remain obedient to his word.

Therefore, as we reflect on the story of the wedding at Cana, we ask ourselves some challenging questions. How do we believe that Jesus is both divine and human? In what ways do we recognise his helping presence in all the circumstances of our various relationships and activities? What about listening to Mary's wise advice to do whatever Jesus tells us? Answering these questions can teach us some valuable lessons from the Cana story.

For meditation
This was the first of the signs given by Jesus: it was given at Cana in Galilee. (JOHN 2:11)

⊕
Third Sunday in Ordinary Time

GOSPEL READING: LUKE 1:1-4; 4:14-21

REFLECTION

We live in an era of manifestos, especially election manifestos from political parties hoping to persuade us to vote for them so that they will be able to implement their vision for society and fulfil their promises. Manifestos generally provide a coherent summary of policies, strategies and evidence which, afterwards, can be used to measure achievements and failures.

In the synagogue at Nazareth, his home town, Jesus presented the manifesto or mission statement for his ministry when he read an extract from the prophet Isaiah and then commented on the text. It referred to being anointed by the Holy Spirit and to preaching the Good News of salvation to the poor. It also prophesied that prisoners and others who were downtrodden would be liberated and that the blind would have their sight restored. According to Isaiah, all these changes would happen with the future coming of the Messiah.

Reading that particular text in the synagogue was not unusual, but Jesus' commentary on the text was truly amazing because he stated clearly that 'this text is being fulfilled today even as you listen' (Luke 4:21). This could only have one meaning: Isaiah's prophecy was being fulfilled there and then in Jesus' person and preaching. In other words, Jesus was the Messiah (that is, the one anointed by God to be the Saviour) for whom generations of God's people had been waiting. The time-of-waiting was now ended.

The implication of Jesus' commentary is that those people who are the least in this world will be the greatest in his new kingdom of peace and justice. There is a well known saying: 'You should always begin as you intend to continue.' Jesus certainly did that as he spoke to his listeners in the synagogue. There, at the outset of his ministry, he told them that he was the Messiah. His mission statement was very clear: 'I am the Messiah.'

The Church continues Jesus' work of bringing the Good News of salvation to the world. The example of his ministry encourages us to be humble in our service as we care for the needy and underprivileged in our society, and as we share the message of God's compassion, forgiveness and healing.

As we begin to listen to extracts from the Gospel of Luke being read during most of the Sundays of the current liturgical year, we know that the time of redemption has come because Jesus the Messiah is finally here. We thank God for sending him. In bringing salvation, he acknowledges the dignity of every human being and teaches that God's grace is equally available to all people.

For meditation

This text is being fulfilled today even as you listen.
(LUKE 4:21)

⊕
Fourth Sunday in Ordinary Time

GOSPEL READING: LUKE 4:21-30

REFLECTION

A prophet's task is never easy. When prophetic people are serious about their task they inevitably become unpopular with other people. Jesus experienced this early in his ministry when he was rejected by the people from his home town. That was why he said: 'No prophet is ever accepted in his own country' (Luke 4:24).

Contrary to much popular opinion, prophets – at least in the biblical understanding of the term – do not foretell the future or speak on their own authority. Throughout Judeo-Christian history, prophets have been first and foremost God's spokespersons, literally people who speak for God. But prophets have also interceded with God on behalf of their people, thereby exercising a dual role in divine-human relationships.

Thus the role of prophets has been, and continues to be, tremendously important and necessary in the lives of God's people. Without prophets, and more particularly without people heeding their teaching, believers in God cannot be knowledgeable about the authentic meaning of his revelation (that is, self-communication).

It is important to realise that prophets emerge from ordinary people, people like us. They do not drop from the sky and they are usually relatively normal people. Indeed, they are reluctant recruits who merely do what is necessary.

This is significant because we tend to dismiss the possibility that we ourselves, or family members, friends or colleagues could be called by God to be prophets in our Church and in the world. The call to be prophetic is part of our baptismal commitment whereby we decide to bear witness to the teaching of Christ and his Church. The fact is that, through the commitment we make in baptism and confirmation, we are obliged to speak the truth, especially when confronted with evil and sinful situations. A question worth answering is: do we accept God's invitation and speak the truth with conviction and true compassion?

Prophets are holy people. They are uncompromising in their faithfulness to the word of God. They always speak the truth, regardless of the consequences, offering encouragement and hope to people who have no sense of meaning or purpose in life. They challenge people to repent for their sins and to seek God's mercy. That is true compassion.

There is still a need for prophets in our society, men and women who are faithful to their baptismal commitment. We need to listen to them and learn from them. Also, we need to remember that every Christian has to exercise the prophetic vocation in the world of work, leisure and family life, praying for the grace to fulfil this important part of our Christian vocation.

For meditation

They took him up to the brow of the hill their town was built on, intending to throw him down the cliff, but he slipped through the crowd and walked away.
(LUKE 4:30)

⊕
Fifth Sunday in Ordinary Time

GOSPEL READING: LUKE 5:1-11

REFLECTION

The account of Jesus calling the fishermen (Simon Peter, James and John) to follow him is not only about them. It is also the story of you and me and all Christian disciples. The fishermen were decisive about abandoning their previous ways of living (we read that 'they left everything and followed him' (Luke 5:11)) and in beginning a new and radically different approach to living. Likewise, we are meant to respond wholeheartedly to Jesus' repeated invitation to follow him.

We are invited to answer Jesus' invitation decisively and publicly, for example, whenever we celebrate the sacraments and when we give public witness to our Christian faith and principles. We also answer his daily invitation in the privacy of our homes, in our work practices and in our ordinary, everyday activities. Thus the task of being a follower of Jesus is unending and we cannot claim holidays or days off. Just as Jesus renews his invitation every day, we renew our response every day.

There is no scope for complacency or self-righteousness on the part of any one of us. Borrowing from the imagery evoked by this invitation, at any given time we may be following him so closely that we think we are almost beside him. Yet he repeats his invitation, never suggesting that we are better than others and that we should rest for a while. We cannot rest from the spiritual life. Seeking Jesus is a constant task.

The opposite may, of course, be our situation. We may not be close to Jesus because our lives are seriously sinful. Nevertheless, he still invites us to follow him. His continuous invitation to sinners is no different from his reminder to those who are saintly. We are all urged to be repentant for our sins, by confessing them humbly when we celebrate God's forgiveness in the sacrament of reconciliation and resolving to avoid sinful occasions and activities in the future. Jesus does not discriminate between people. Although he loves each one of us uniquely, he treats us equally.

Following Jesus involves devoting our whole lives to him and his teaching. This is what conversion is about. It means total commitment to the Good News and thus to a new way of living. Following Jesus means entering into a personal relationship of friendship with him. In baptismal terms it means becoming his brothers and sisters.

How do we respond to Jesus' daily invitation to follow him? We can answer 'Yes' only if we are seriously trying to be faithful to his teaching and the teaching of his Church. Following Jesus, being a disciple, is demanding. It requires letting the teaching of Jesus and his Church inform all our routine decisions in addition to the major choices we make during life. After genuinely answering 'Yes' to his call, our lives – like those of Simon Peter, James and John, his first disciples – will never again be the same because we will dedicate ourselves completely to doing

God's will. We pray that we may always be faithful to Jesus' call and that we will lead others to do the same.

For meditation
They left everything and followed him. (LUKE 5:11)

⊕
Sixth Sunday in Ordinary Time

GOSPEL READING: LUKE 6:17, 20-26

REFLECTION

This may seem to be a strange question: how happy are we and what makes us happy? Many people associate happiness with the things of this life: money and possessions, power and fame. But material wealth and adulation do not bring permanent happiness. Often they become sources of great unhappiness in our lives. Many of us search for happiness in vain because we seek it in places and activities where it cannot be found.

Happiness is really an attitude of heart. Christians can be truly happy only when our relationship with God is humble and trusting. God is the ultimate source of our happiness because, unlike the often short-lived pleasures of earthly fame and material possessions, God offers us contentment in this life and eternal happiness in the next life.

However, contentment in this life and eternal happiness in the next life do not just happen without any effort on our part. We have to work for contentment and happiness. The beatitudes provide us with a formula for happiness – happiness that only God can promise and guarantee. They present us with demanding challenges, for example, being poor in spirit, being hungry and weeping. But they also encourage us with corresponding rewards or assurances, for instance, the kingdom of God, satisfaction and a guarantee of laughter. Indeed, our reward will be great in heaven because God cares especially for those who are lowly and oppressed.

Thus the beatitudes offer us a framework for daily Christian living so that we can imitate the teaching and example of Jesus. They also provide us with hope because they teach us about what awaits us in return for our faithfulness to the challenges of the Good News.

The beatitudes teach us to become humble and simple in our lifestyles so that we are not distracted from the real purpose of life by the false promises of this world. When we are preoccupied with the trappings of success or wealth, we are unable to recognise our total dependence on God because we think that we can exist without God. In contrast, humility and simplicity enable us to be open to God's loving presence so that we can live contented and happy lives.

If a secular version of the beatitudes was being written by some of today's great thinkers, it might read: 'Happy are those who rise to the top in their profession: they will have two houses. Happy are those who win the national lottery: they will be the envy of other people.' But such transient happiness, based as it is on self-interest rather than selflessness, is not true happiness. It does not bring inner peace of mind and definitely does not lead to eternity.

Therefore, we need a change of attitude. The beatitudes invite us to be simple in our living, in the way that Jesus was. They challenge us to focus on what matters most – proper attitudes and dispositions, not earthly riches and possessions. We listen attentively again to the words of Jesus: 'Happy are you when people hate you, drive you out, abuse you, denounce your name as criminal, on account of the Son of Man.

Rejoice when that day comes and dance for joy, for then your reward will be great in heaven' (Luke 6:21-22).

For meditation

How happy are you who are poor; yours is the kingdom of heaven. Alas for you who are rich; you are having your consolation now. (LUKE 6:20, 24)

⊕
Seventh Sunday in Ordinary Time

GOSPEL READING: LUKE 6:27-38

REFLECTION

Like every good teacher, Jesus communicated with his disciples on several different levels. Sometimes, he wanted them to interpret his words literally. For instance, he taught them: 'Love your enemies, do good to those who hate you, bless those who curse you, pray for those who treat you badly' (Luke 6:27-28). Jesus intended his disciples, including us, to adhere strictly to those words. We know this because he always practiced what he preached, especially when he was dying on the cross.

One of the central features of Christianity is the love of enemies. Loving our enemies and praying for those who treat us badly require great personal sacrifices from us. Yet we cannot claim to be genuine disciples of Jesus if we are unwilling to make such sacrifices. We are challenged by Jesus' teaching and example to treat others as we would like them to treat us, regardless of how they behave towards us. We need to be compassionate as our heavenly Father is compassionate.

However, a literal interpretation of the sayings of Jesus does not extend to such phrases as 'To the man who slaps you on one cheek, present the other cheek too; to the man who takes your cloak from you, do not refuse your tunic' (Luke 6:29). To do so would be missing the message. In this instance Jesus was speaking in a deliberately exaggerated manner. In other words, there is no useful purpose in endlessly turning the other cheek and in giving away all our clothes until we have none for ourselves. This would be futile and crazy.

Sometimes, instead of requiring his disciples to understand his teaching literally, Jesus deliberately overstated the case so that he would convey the underlying principle in his argument. Actually, such an exaggerated form of speech was commonly used by religious and moral teachers during Jesus' life and ministry.

Often the kernel of his argument is that we should reflect on our attitudes and dispositions, because our motivation for action is influenced ultimately by our prevailing attitudes and dispositions. Therefore, if we wish to change our behaviour, we need to focus on the underlying motivation and not on the behaviour itself.

So what is Jesus' message? It is a challenge to examine the inner motivation for what we say and how we behave. A superficial reflection on our actions is never sufficient for Christians because it does not result in any radical change. Radical change in our behaviour – which is the kind of change demanded by the Good News – occurs only when the underlying attitudes and dispositions governing that behaviour are changed. Jesus hoped that, by overstating his position, his disciples would begin to realise this and permit such fundamental change to happen in their lives. This is the key to understanding Jesus' moral teaching.

We are challenged to evaluate our commitment to the Good News by examining the underlying attitudes and dispositions which decide how we behave. It is our attitudes and dispositions, which are always precursory to our behaviour, that lead us to sin. The standard by which we are judged is on whether or not our motives, not our actions, are sincere. We would all do well to take note.

For meditation
Be compassionate as your Father is compassionate.
(LUKE 6:36)

⊕

Eighth Sunday in Ordinary Time

GOSPEL READING: LUKE 6:39-45

REFLECTION

How would we feel if our neighbours or colleagues spoke about us to other people and said to them: 'Those people are hypocrites.' Would we feel hurt, embarrassed or angry? Or would we be indifferent and ignore their comment?

Most of us would be upset and angry if such comments were made about us because we would resent being described in such a manner. More significantly, we would disagree with what was being said because we do not think that we are hypocrites. We instinctively assume that we do not exercise double standards.

Yet Jesus did not hesitate to speak directly to his disciples about hypocrisy. He said: 'Why do you observe the splinter in your brother's eye and never notice the plank in your own? How can you say to your brother, "Brother, let me take out the splinter that is in your eye", when you cannot see the plank in your own? Hypocrite! Take the plank out of your own eye first, and then you will see clearly enough to take out the splinter that is in your brother's eye' (Luke 6:41-42).

Could Jesus rightly describe us as hypocrites? Hypocrites are nasty people. They are full of self-importance. They are arrogant, smug and self-righteous, lacking humility and sensitivity. They revel in other people's misfortune. Fundamentally, their behaviour differs from their words.

They exercise double standards, often imposing unachievable tasks and demanding rules on other people while applying far less strict standards and rules to themselves. They are harsh and dismissive in their attitudes and they rarely offer people a second chance. In summary, they make life very difficult for other people. Unfortunately, our world and our Church have many hypocrites.

The reasons Jesus challenged his disciples about hypocrisy were obvious. He observed how they treated other people. He noticed that they lacked sincerity. He knew them better than they knew themselves. Self-righteous people become so focused on other people's faults and mistakes that they are unable to recognise and accept their own shortcomings.

The same can be true about us. Other people, including Jesus, know us far better than we know ourselves. They recognise the double standards in our lives because they are frequently the victims of our self-righteousness and stern judgements, to which we are often oblivious. They could well say to us with considerable justification: 'Take the plank out of your own eye first.'

Jesus' teaching compels us to root out the hypocrisy from our lives. The lesson is clear: there is no role for double standards in the life of sincere Christians.

For meditation

A man's words flow out of what fills his heart.
(LUKE 6:45)

⊕
Ninth Sunday in Ordinary Time

GOSPEL READING: LUKE 7:1-10

REFLECTION

In reflecting on the story about Jesus and the Roman centurion in Capernaum, we learn much about both of them that may help us to live better lives. What is most surprising, of course, is that there was any contact between them because, normally, Jews did not associate in any way with Gentiles (Jesus was a Jew and the centurion was a Gentile).

The centurion was obviously a special kind of human being and, undoubtedly, this contributed to the successful outcome of their communication, which was mediated through some Jewish elders. Fundamentally, as Jesus acknowledged, the centurion had great faith.

In particular, he expressed a confident faith in Jesus. Although a Gentile, he was receptive to God's grace and help, unlike many of the Jews who had rejected Jesus' message. He demonstrated his faith by his belief that it was not necessary to meet Jesus physically in order to ask for healing, and that Jesus could heal his dying servant without seeing him. Jesus only had to 'give the word' (Luke 7:7) and the servant would recover. It is no wonder, then, that Jesus said: 'I tell you, not even in Israel have I found faith like this' (Luke 7:9).

The centurion demonstrated genuine humility, although he was, himself, a man of authority. He did not presume to approach Jesus directly but, instead, asked some Jewish elders to speak to Jesus on his behalf, respecting the fact that Jews did not deal with Gentiles. Even the centurion's humble phrase, 'I am not worthy to have you under my roof' (Luke 7:6) has been incorporated into our prayers before receiving Holy Communion whenever we celebrate the Eucharist.

But the story teaches us much about Jesus too. It becomes clear that Jesus' mission of bringing salvation was not confined to the Jewish people. By healing a foreigner's servant, he indicated that his Good News of salvation is for everyone. From Jesus' perspective, there are no Gentiles. All people are equal – in the sense that God's love and compassion are equally available to everyone.

A central theme in Luke's Gospel is the universality of God's salvation. The Church continues the saving work of Christ and is thus the sign of salvation to the entire world. Therefore, when we think about the Church's catholicity, which is one of its four distinguishing characteristics, we are reminded that God's salvation in and through Christ our Saviour is for all people of every time and place. For Christ, there are no outsiders, which is the moral of the encounter between Jesus and the Roman centurion in Capernaum and the subsequent healing of the centurion's servant.

For meditation

I tell you, not even in Israel have I found faith like this. (LUKE 7:9)

⊕
Tenth Sunday in Ordinary Time

GOSPEL READING: LUKE 7:11-17

REFLECTION

The story about the widow of Nain and her dead son is only recorded in Luke's Gospel. The miracle worked by Jesus involved bringing a dead man back to life. Whatever about curing people's illnesses and casting out demons – and there are many such incidents in the gospels – restoring life to a dead person is truly amazing. Only God can do this. By raising the widow's son to life, Jesus was making clear to the 'great number of people' (Luke 7:11) who witnessed this miracle that he was no ordinary, merely human, person.

We need to understand this miracle in the same way as Jesus' other miracles. It is important to realise that the miracles are signs that Jesus was sent by God and that he is in the same line as all the great prophets who were sent before him. (Many of the ancient prophets had also done miraculous deeds.) But Jesus is much more than a prophet. He is the Lord, the Son of God. He is even referred to by Luke as 'the Lord' (Luke 7:13), a title that is reserved for the glorious Christ.

This is particularly evident in the raising to life of the widow's dead son. Both the giving of life and the taking of life belong to God alone. In this incident, Jesus, unlike some of the ancient prophets like Elijah who interceded with God to restore life, used his own power to raise the dead man: 'Young man, I tell you to get up' (Luke 7:14).

Thus Jesus' word is the source of life, especially spiritual life. In giving back her son to the grieving widow, Jesus proved that God is willing to intervene in human situations to display his merciful love.

This miracle was a spectacular sign that God was working in and through Jesus' actions. When the people witnessed what Jesus had done, they were astonished and said: 'A great prophet has appeared among us; God has visited his people' (Luke 7:16). This clear statement expressed their belief that Jesus was not just another prophet but the actual presence of God among his people.

The true humanity of Jesus is also found in the story of the widow of Nain. It was Jesus' sympathy for her tragic predicament that initially engaged him in her circumstances. But, almost immediately, his compassion becomes the vehicle for God to work directly in this human situation, bringing life and health.

The practical challenge, from reflecting on this miracle story, is to be convinced about God's merciful love and to be sensitive to the difficulties of those who are less fortunate than ourselves. God is indeed compassionate, and Jesus is proof that God has visited his people. Just as the crowd who witnessed the widow's dead son being brought back to life instantly recognised that this was the work of God, so we, too, strive to recognise God working, albeit perhaps less dramatically, in the events of our own daily lives. God was close to the widow of Nain and he is also close to each one of us.

For meditation

Young man, I tell you to get up. (LUKE 7:15)

⊕
Eleventh Sunday in Ordinary Time

GOSPEL READING: LUKE 7:36–8:3

REFLECTION

The practice of forgiveness is essential to Christianity. If we do not forgive ourselves and others, we will be unwilling or unable to appreciate God's forgiveness. This, in turn, means that we will never be truly happy and content. It also means that we will be unable to receive God's forgiveness.

Jesus taught that 'the amount you measure out is the amount you will be given' (Mark 4:24). Therefore we are required to forgive others to the extent that we hope to be forgiven ourselves – by others and by God. And yet, forgiveness is the most difficult task in our lives because it requires us to let go of the hurt that is often deeply rooted.

We know that Jesus was 'a friend of sinners' (Luke 7:34). When he visited the home of Simon the Pharisee for a meal, he shocked Simon and the other people there when he said to the woman who arrived unexpectedly and anointed his feet with ointment: 'Your sins are forgiven' (Luke 7:48). Jesus treated the woman who had a bad reputation in the same way that he treated all sinners: he readily forgave her sins.

Occasionally, unlike God, we refuse to forgive. We may say to another person: 'Maybe God forgives you, but I do not forgive you.' Or we may say to ourselves: 'Perhaps God forgives me, but I don't.' So we acknowledge that God gladly forgives sinners while, at the same time, stating that we refuse to do so.

This is a very dangerous scenario because, when we engage in it, we risk committing a most serious sin.

The logical conclusion of such a stance is that we have higher or more exacting standards than God. If that is so, the implication is that we are greater than God, which is tantamount to saying that God is subservient to us. We make ourselves into false gods, thereby breaking the first commandment as well as infringing Jesus' instruction to forgive our neighbour continually (see Matthew 18:21-22).

Sometimes we think that, unless we forget whatever was said or done that hurt us, we have not forgiven. But forgiveness is about an act of the will – it has nothing to do with the emotions which may remain. And it is not necessarily about forgetting the hurt caused. Forgiveness is about deciding not to be controlled any longer by the effects of the hurt, and not to nurture the grievance which only makes us bitter and angry.

On a spiritual level, forgiving means recognising that nothing we suffer in this life is equivalent to what Christ, who was totally innocent, suffered and died to secure our salvation. By uniting our sufferings with his suffering, we strengthen our character and our souls. Only then will we be really free people, because only then will we be able to think about or be in the presence of those who have offended us without allowing their damaging behaviour to cause further hurt.

The reality is that it is easy for God to forgive sinners because he loves us. We are challenged by the Good News of salvation to imitate God's desire to forgive. As people who are forgiven, we are called to be forgiving towards ourselves and others. If we refuse to forgive, then we will be unable to value forgiveness when it is offered to us from other people and God. We pray, then, that we will be gracious in accepting forgiveness when it is offered and that we will be generous in forgiving others.

For meditation
Her sins, her many sins, must have been forgiven her, or she would not have shown such great love. (LUKE 7:47)

⊕
Twelfth Sunday in Ordinary Time

GOSPEL READING: LUKE 9:18-24

REFLECTION

Jesus once asked his disciples: 'Who do the crowds say I am?' (Luke 9:18). They replied: 'John the Baptist, others Elijah; and others say one of the ancient prophets come back to life' (Luke 9:19). It is easy to speculate generally about other people and their opinions. However, it is often much more challenging to be specific about ourselves when the attention is on us.

Who do we say that Jesus is? This is a central question regarding the fundamentals of the Christian faith. It challenges us to know what we claim to believe as Christians and, after prayerful reflection, to reaffirm our belief in Jesus the Messiah, the Son of the living God. Without any doubt, the answer to Jesus' question 'Who do you say that I am?' is: Jesus Christ is the universal Saviour, our Lord and God. For example, Peter's answer was: 'The Christ of God' (Luke 9:20), that is, the Messiah, the Anointed One.

Unfortunately, however, we often answer the question 'Who do you say that I am?' by using well-rehearsed phrases that, while theoretically correct, have not been internalised because they have not arisen from our personal experience of the Lordship of Jesus Christ in our lives. There is a vast difference between knowing about Jesus Christ and knowing him personally – in the same way that there is a significant difference between knowing about a colleague at work and knowing that person personally. During Jesus' earthly ministry, many people who knew about him did not know him personally. Sadly, that situation has remained unchanged today.

Human civilisation is, in one sense, advancing greatly. Our ideas and our language are increasingly sophisticated. We live in a rapidly expanding information age. Yet, in another sense, our civilisation is slowly but surely disintegrating. It lacks meaning and a definite purpose.

Traditional values and well-established principles are being abandoned. For many people, the name of Jesus Christ is just another piece of the huge jigsaw of knowledge and information. His name is not acknowledged as unique in the history of humankind. Indeed, his name is frequently used blasphemously. In such a culture, Christians are losing their sense of identity.

Our identity is rooted in Christ Jesus, the Lord of the universe and Saviour of humankind. At baptism we became brothers and sisters in Christ, co-heirs to the kingdom of God. If we acknowledge seriously the baptismal dignity that is ours, then we can never ask 'Who am I?' without simultaneously asking 'Who is Jesus for me?' Our true identity can only be found in the salvation he has won for us by his suffering and death.

We need to 'go back to basics'. Who is Jesus for us? What words and phrases do we use when describing his significance in our lives? Do those words merely communicate knowledge about him or do they communicate a deeply personal relationship with him that acknowledges him as the only Son of the living God? We need to be wary about using language that sounds attractive but actually means nothing because it has not been internalised. Let us avoid making the mistake of knowing about Jesus Christ while not knowing him personally.

For meditation

'But you,' he said, 'who do you say I am?' It was Peter who spoke up. 'The Christ of God,' he said.
(LUKE 9:20)

⊕
Thirteenth Sunday in Ordinary Time

GOSPEL READING: LUKE 9:51-62

REFLECTION

In Luke's Gospel we read about a man who, meeting Jesus on the road, said to him: 'I will follow you wherever you go' (Luke 9:57). What a vote of confidence in Jesus. What a commitment the man was making. It was nothing less than total. Then Jesus explained that such a commitment could not be given lightly. Commitment to following him would necessitate single-mindedness and dedication. It would require much more than merely following him. It would demand a personal conviction and faithfulness to his teaching. And last but not least, it would be life-long.

Did we ever make a total and life-long commitment to Jesus? In effect, did we say to him: 'I will follow you wherever you go?' The short answer, whether we realise it or not, is 'Yes'. The hope, of course, is that we are acutely aware of it every day.

Most of us will not have said to Jesus explicitly: 'I will follow you wherever you go.' Nonetheless, we gave that commitment on several occasions. One such time was the commitment made on behalf of each one of us by our parents and god-parents when we were baptised. Similarly, we ourselves renewed that commitment when we celebrated the sacrament of confirmation. Those of us who are married committed ourselves completely to the person and teaching of Jesus again when we committed ourselves to our spouses 'for better for worse, for richer for poorer, in sickness and in health, all the days of our lives'.

The commitment we make at baptism, confirmation and marriage – which, if we are faithful, is total and life-long – parallels the irrevocable commitment that God has made to us, especially in sending his Son into the world. Jesus' commitment to us was so complete that he suffered and died on the cross to save us from the consequences of our sins. Regrettably, we break our commitment to Jesus every time we sin.

We renew that commitment every day as we speak and behave in accordance with the teaching of Christ and his Church. We also do so whenever we receive Christ's forgiveness in the sacrament of reconciliation.

In his teaching, Jesus was very clear about the kind of commitment he expects. He said: 'Once the hand is laid on the plough, no one who looks back is fit for the kingdom of God' (Luke 9:62). Strong words indeed. So the commitments that we initially embrace enthusiastically and with determination need to be continued as we have begun them. This applies particularly to our Christian faith.

At the heart of Christ's teaching is the invitation to make a commitment to him. 'Follow me' (Luke 5:27): Jesus says this to us every day of our lives. Do we follow Christ at all times, even when colleagues and friends confront us with ideas and lifestyles that contradict his teaching? Furthermore, do we follow Christ in our daily relationships by challenging the cultural changes that have become accepted in our society despite the fact that they flout his great commandments to love God and to love our neighbour? Our baptismal commitment requires us to renounce the Devil and his temptations.

Jesus asks us to make a total commitment to him. This may seem strange in an age when many people no longer have any sense of what it means to make a permanent commitment. Nevertheless, true Christian discipleship is based on a total and permanent commitment. A good principle for Christian living is to continue the commitment to Jesus that we made in baptism, resolving to follow him wherever he goes.

For meditation

[Jesus] resolutely took the road for Jerusalem.
As they travelled along they met a man on the road
who said to him, 'I will follow you wherever you go'.
(LUKE 9:51, 57)

⊕
Fourteenth Sunday in Ordinary Time

GOSPEL READING: LUKE 10:1-12, 17-20

REFLECTION
When Jesus sent the seventy-two disciples out ahead of him in pairs, he instructed them to tell those

people who would not welcome them: 'We wipe off the very dust of your town that clings to our feet, and leave it with you' (Luke 10:11). Strange words indeed!

On reading these words, they may initially seem rather harsh. Would they not be likely to cause further trouble where the disciples were already unwelcome? Would they not be considered to be offensive and insulting?

However, as with all of Jesus' words, there was no intention to be disrespectful and insensitive even if, at times, they were very direct. Instead, while also referring to the consequences for those who would reject his teaching, Jesus was teaching his disciples another important principle. Whenever others would not welcome them because they rejected Jesus' message, the disciples should not allow the rejection or hardness of heart that fuelled the lack of welcome to prevent them proclaiming the nearness of God's kingdom.

Jesus advised his disciples not to pick up unnecessary and damaging baggage from the negative reactions of people to their efforts to be faithful to his teaching and to share it freely. He taught them to ignore the cynical attitudes and unhelpful comments they would encounter just like they would wipe off the dust of rejection clinging to their feet. Otherwise, they could easily become disillusioned and lose their enthusiasm and single-mindedness.

Resentment and cynicism would slow them down metaphorically just as dust on their feet would slow them down physically. Basically, Jesus told his disciples not to be influenced by the anger and hostility they would occasionally experience as they taught and preached the Good News.

There is an indispensable lesson here for us: being faithful to the teaching of Christ and his Church is not popular. Commitment to the Good News frequently brings scorn and smart comments. It is thought to be irrelevant. When we speak the truth and live according to the Commandments, we are often dismissed as being too old-fashioned.

Unfaithfulness – in every sense of the word – and dishonesty are rampant in our society. God and the Church are increasingly perceived as redundant. Many people claim that they are meaningless. In such circumstances it is difficult for those of us who are committed Christians to remain resolute in our convictions and it is an appealing temptation simply to 'go with the flow'. Choosing that option would, ultimately, be worthless.

The challenge for us is never to be abusive or retaliatory when we are rejected by family and friends because of our beliefs. Two wrongs never make a right. We need to remain faithful to the teaching of Christ and his Church and continue to be credible witnesses by what we think and say and do. When, in the face of adversity, we do what we know and believe to be correct, we may have to wipe off the dust that clings to our feet and rejoice that our names are written in heaven.

For meditation

And if a man of peace lives there, your peace will go and rest on him; if not, it will come back to you.
(LUKE 10:6)

⊕
Fifteenth Sunday in Ordinary Time

GOSPEL READING: LUKE 10:1-12, 17-20

REFLECTION

The familiar parable of the good Samaritan was Jesus' response to the fundamental question: who is my neighbour? Jesus, being a wise moral educator, often answered questions by telling parables or stories. He then concluded with his own question. Thus Jesus gently guided the questioner to discover the truth within the answer to the original question. In this way he encouraged his audiences to think through his teachings.

The parable of the good Samaritan contains some interesting characters. Quite apart from the brigands – from whom we would expect no respect or compassion – the reactions of the priest and Levite to the plight of the injured man are disappointing. Neither of them was prepared to stop and help him. No doubt they had excuses, but there can never be any justification for ignoring an injured person whose life is in danger. Their unconcern, especially as people whose religious practice was ostensibly central in their lives, indicated a lack of compassion for other people in times of suffering.

Like the lawyer in the gospel reading, having listened to the parable, each one of us knows instinctively the correct answer to the question: who is my neighbour? It is obvious! We cannot limit our understanding of neighbour to the person who lives next door to us. All people, particularly those needing material and spiritual help, are our neighbours, just as all other Christians are our brothers and sisters in Christ.

Often the lesson of the parable of the good Samaritan is interpreted narrowly as applying only to material needs. However, Christ's teachings always point to eternal values. Putting into practice the teaching of Christ and his Church in its fullness enables us to reach out to people who might otherwise not have the possibility of considering that teaching and its life-giving message of hope. Regrettably, for various reasons, many of us fail to do this. Effectively, we pass by on the other side (see Luke 10:32).

The challenge, then, for us is to realise that there needs to be consistency between what we say, on the one hand, and what we do, on the other. Most of us know the correct answers to the fundamental questions in life, particularly about our responsibilities towards others. But we do not always put these answers into practice. This was true of both the priest and the Levite in the parable. In contrast, the Samaritan, who was considered to be very much a second-class citizen, knew the correct thing to do. More significantly, he did it.

Each one of us has within ourselves the ability to judge what is correct. During his public ministry, Jesus often demonstrated that the answers to the questions about what is right and what is wrong are already in our minds and hearts. This is because, if our consciences are correctly formed, we can recognise the moral and religious truths revealed to us by God.

Basically, in the parable of the good Samaritan we are invited to recognise what it means to be a neighbour and to respond accordingly, just as the Samaritan responded. Thus we are challenged to 'go, and do the same' (Luke 10:37).

For meditation

And who is my neighbour? (LUKE 10:29)

⊕
Sixteenth Sunday in Ordinary Time

Gospel reading: Luke 10:38-42

Reflection

Sometimes, although we do not always realise it, we use avoidance tactics in our relationships with other people and with God. We can be quite uncomfortable simply being with another person, for whatever reason. To avoid this, we often rush around doing many things to help and please, in an apparently generous fashion. We cannot cope with the silence. Therefore, we prefer the distraction of some activity.

Jesus experienced this when he visited the home of Martha and Mary. They were hospitable in different ways. After Martha had welcomed Jesus she became busy serving, whereas Mary just sat at his feet and listened to him speaking.

Martha of necessity had to be busy. If Jesus had to depend on Mary preparing a meal, he would have had a long wait. Thus both Martha and Mary had different roles to play. However, Martha thought that Mary was inconsiderate and lazy, and she complained to Jesus that she had to do all the work.

Jesus' response surprised her. He said: 'Martha, Martha, you worry and fret about so many things, and yet few are needed, indeed only one. It is Mary who has chosen the better part; it is not to be taken from her' (Luke 10:41-42). Essentially, Jesus told Martha that she was not really being present to him. He would have preferred if, like Mary, she sat and chatted or that she would listen and chat while she worked. He hoped that Martha would have been more communicative like Mary who had given him her full attention.

It is easy for us to step into Martha's shoes and become preoccupied with matters that are of secondary importance. In doing this, we become too busy to listen and, subsequently, we feel aggrieved when the person appreciates other people, although these people seem to be doing nothing.

Mary did what, for many of us, is most difficult. She responded to Jesus' presence by simply being with him as she sat and listened. The important lesson for us is that, while it is commendable to do things for other people, the doing of these things cannot become a legitimate substitute for caring for their souls. Therefore, when we next meet someone who, for example, is ill or lonely or visiting us, we will simply be with that person. We will sit and respond by listening and sharing ourselves.

The same applies to our relationship with God. Often we clutter it with many distractions. We cannot bear silence, so the thought of simply sitting and listening to God is frightening. Instead we engage in various forms of frenetic activity because such activity numbs our discomfort. So we say some memorised prayers, we sing hymns and we watch processions – without our souls being still and peaceful.

While all these sacred activities are important in our worship of God, there also needs to be time for silence. If we do not sit and listen with our souls at least occasionally, we do not let God into our lives. For instance, it is amusing to notice the inability of people gathered at Sunday Mass to sit still for silent prayer and reflection. If the priest incorporates a few moments of silence after the distribution of Holy Communion, it is usually quickly broken by people coughing and shuffling their feet.

We need to remember that there are different kinds of hospitality. Sometimes it is more important to 'be' rather than to 'do'. This is how we give our full attention to Jesus.

For meditation
It is Mary who has chosen the better part; it is not to be taken from her. (LUKE 10:42)

⊕
Seventeenth Sunday in Ordinary Time

GOSPEL READING: LUKE 11:1-13

REFLECTION

We often talk about the power of prayer and, especially in desperate situations, we admit that when all else fails we can still pray for consolation and peace of mind. Most of us readily acknowledge that prayer is one of the main characteristics of true Christian discipleship.

Throughout his life, Jesus persisted in praying to his heavenly Father. The four gospels recount how he always prayed before making important decisions and whenever he experienced crises while proclaiming the nearness of God's kingdom. Even when he was tired, he still found time to pray.

Indeed it was the example of Jesus at prayer that inspired the disciples to ask him to teach them how to pray. His response has traditionally been known as 'the Lord's Prayer' and it expresses intimacy and trust between God and whoever is praying, whether an individual or a community. Such intimacy and trust are essential to good communication.

Communication is at the heart of sincere prayer – communication that is a dialogue between two persons. Thus when Jesus taught his disciples how to pray, he taught them how to engage in conversation with God. Also, he stressed the need to persevere in this conversation.

When we communicate with God through praying, we learn much from God. For example, we learn about who God is and what his will is for us. Sometimes God's will is not immediately obvious. Occasionally we resist God's will because it asks us to curb our selfish desires and abandon our sins. Then, of course, there are times when it seems that God does not answer our prayers.

Jesus challenges us to trust God and to be persistent in our prayer. He assures us that, when we persist, God responds with generosity and mercy. Hence prayer is fundamental to our relationships with God.

Significantly, as Jesus teaches us how to pray, he tells us that our heavenly Father will always give the Holy Spirit to those who ask. The greatest gift that God gives us is the Spirit because the Spirit enlivens and empowers us.

Throughout the Christian centuries, the Church has developed and promoted many different approaches to prayer. These approaches appeal to different personalities and temperaments. But all genuine approaches are the work of the Holy Spirit.

Why should we persist in praying for the gift of the Holy Spirit? By becoming more attentive to the prompting of the Spirit we will be able to sustain and strengthen our hope in the goodness of God at all times. Without the Spirit there cannot be complete unity among Christians and the Church lacks credibility. We need to pray especially that the Spirit will guide and lead the Church in these times of confusion and uncertainty. We persist in praying for the gift of the Spirit.

The real power of prayer is that it opens our eyes to the mystery of God. Knowing that God is always near and willing to help us in every situation, we become ready for God to use us to do great things in his name. Prayer sustains our hope that God will never abandon us and, through the Holy Spirit, will guide us to the truth and to eternal life.

In faith, therefore, let us ask so that we will receive. Let us search so that we will find and let us knock so that the door will be opened to us. May the example of Jesus at prayer inspire us to persist in prayer.

For meditation

Ask, and it will be given you; search, and you will find; knock, and the door will be opened to you. (LUKE 11:9)

⊕
Eighteenth Sunday in Ordinary Time

GOSPEL READING: LUKE 12:13-21

REFLECTION

Are we rich in God's sight or, because of how we live, are we poor? This is an important question to ask ourselves occasionally as we reflect on our relationships with God and other people.

The Good News challenges us to focus on our true priorities and values. We live in a sophisticated world. Until recently, the economy was booming and our culture applauds materialism and success. The acquisitive nature of many people manifests itself in such things as second family cars that are often unnecessary, televisions in every room in the home and instant achievements. As a result of Original Sin, our fallen human nature means that we are naturally inclined to be selfish and we need God's grace to overcome that selfishness.

We can become so preoccupied in living for the present – and in storing up short-term wealth and possessions – that our long-term priorities and values are forgotten. Frequently, the quality of our lives, in terms of time and relationships, does not improve and we are not any happier. Even our relationship with God is put on hold and we no longer appreciate the relevance of the Church in our everyday lives. When life is going well and we seem to be in control of our destiny, many people argue that God does not exist and that there is no need for the Church.

This temptation, like all temptations, comes from the Devil and not, as some people suggest, from our more 'adult' psychology. We must remember that God made us to know, love and serve him in this world so that we will be happy with him forever in heaven.

Significantly, Jesus reminds us about the stark reality that we are not completely in control of our lives. In the parable about the rich man with the good harvest, God says to him: 'Fool! This very night the demand will be made for your soul; and this hoard of yours, whose will it be then?' (Luke 12:20). This is a clear indication that our souls are more important than material wealth.

Jesus challenges us to re-examine our priorities and values. The parable of the rich man with the good harvest teaches us to avoid greed and recognise that there is more to life than our possessions. Importantly, the parable is a reminder that we are not to store up goods in this world. At the end of our earthly lives we will be accountable for our souls and how we used the graces available to us. Then it will not matter how much money we saved or how many cars we owned.

We may think that we can live for the present without reference to God and respect for people. We may even think that we will have the opportunities to rekindle and restore proper relationships with God and other people at a later time. However, for some of us there will not be a later time. Jesus reminds us: 'So it is when a man stores up treasure for himself in place of making himself rich in the sight of God' (Luke 12:21). Our values and priorities need to be based on the teaching of Christ and his Church.

So the time to act is NOW and the question to answer is: what comes first: our souls' relationships with God or our personal relationships with material goods and our selfish desires?

For meditation
This hoard of yours, whose will it be then? (LUKE 12:20)

⊕
Nineteenth Sunday in Ordinary Time

GOSPEL READING: LUKE 12:32-48

REFLECTION

Jesus told the parable of the servants waiting for their master's return so that he could teach his disciples to be ready to meet him whenever he would come into their lives. Jesus' coming into their lives many times on this earth was a preparation for their final meeting with him in death.

Basically, his message was that, if they did not recognise and accept him in this life – like many of their contemporaries, especially the religious leaders – they would not suddenly recognise and welcome him when they died. Then it would be impossible for them to undo a lifetime's carelessness, indifference and laziness. Instead, Jesus advised them to be like servants who were always prepared for their master's return. The disciples needed to be vigilant.

We, too, are asked to cultivate the virtue of vigilance regarding the coming of Jesus into our lives and activities. We need to have an expectant attitude of listening and watching while we wait for Christ to come. In practice, he comes into our lives in many different ways and in many different people every day. Also, we will surely meet him in death. Therefore, in his words: 'See that you are dressed for action and have your lamps lit because the Son of Man is coming at an hour you do not expect' (Luke 12:35, 40).

We meet Jesus most personally and intimately when we receive his Body and Blood in Holy Communion. We also encounter him whenever his word is proclaimed and in the Church's teaching, which offers us clear guidance about how to live. But we meet Jesus, too, in the words spoken by other people in true charity, and in their smiles.

These people are often strangers who, initially, may seem to have no attractive qualities. Thus we have the possibility of meeting him in the often unexpected and strange situations and people of daily life. If we do not avail of such opportunities, disaster looms. Jesus reminds us that 'the servant who knows what his master wants, but has not even started to carry out those wishes, will receive very many strokes of the lash' (Luke 12:47).

'Practice makes perfect' is a well known saying. It summarises Jesus' message in the parable about the waiting servants. In seeking to meet Jesus in other people, and by joyfully embracing the tasks of everyday living, our efforts will be perfected and we will be adequately prepared to welcome him when he finally comes at the end of our earthly lives. If we work at recognising Jesus in life's various opportunities, he will recognise us and lead us to heaven.

Celebrating the sacrament of reconciliation helps us to be vigilant. If we are sincere in examining our consciences and humble in accepting God's forgiveness, we are indeed undergoing conversion. Our ongoing conversion ensures that we remain in the state of grace (that is, sharing God's life). This is important because, with an increasing loss of the sense of sin, some people arrogantly presume that God is lucky to have them rather than humbly pray for God's mercy.

A question for us, then, is: are we prepared and ready to meet Christ whenever and however he comes? In other words, are we vigilant as we wait for the Lord's coming? Because we have been given much, much will be expected of us.

For meditation
You too must stand ready. (LUKE 12:40)

⊕
Twentieth Sunday in Ordinary Time

GOSPEL READING: LUKE 12:49-53

REFLECTION

'Do you suppose that I am here to bring peace on earth? No, I tell you, but rather division' (Luke 12:51).

In order to understand these words of Jesus, we need to consider what follows them in the gospel reading: 'For from now on a household of five will be divided: three against two and two against three; the father divided against the son, son against father, mother against daughter, daughter against mother, mother-in-law against daughter-in-law, daughter-in-law against mother-in-law' (Luke 12:52-53).

With these words, Jesus explains to us that his teaching is of paramount importance. If we are truly committed to him and his way of life, then we can love nothing and no one – even those naturally closest to us, our families – more than we love him and the truth he teaches. Jesus is warning us not to confuse true and false understandings of peace. It is only by reconciling our lives to the truths of his teaching and the teaching of his Church that we will discover true peace, a peace that the world cannot give.

We all yearn for peace in our own lives, especially peace of mind and heart. Many of us pray for peace in our families, communities, country and throughout the world. And yet, the society in which we live and the world in general never needed peace more than at this time.

On the daily news, we are bombarded with reports of violence, aggression, conflict, tribulation and war in so many parts of the world. Sadly, our own country is not immune from strife and conflict. We live and work in an increasingly violent and dangerous environment that is desperately in need of peace.

The Hebrew word for peace is *shalom*. In its fullest sense, *shalom* is not limited to the absence of hostility. Such a narrow understanding is impoverished. *Shalom* has much more positive and broader shades of meaning. The essential meaning of *shalom* emphasises harmony, integrity, wholesomeness, health, success and, significantly, oneness or unity. Thus it refers to a whole way of living rather than simply describing the absence of hatred and aggression.

Therefore, praying for peace means more than praying for the absence of violence. It means praying for a new way of living that is fundamentally based on harmony and unity with God and within ourselves ever before we think about integrity and wholesomeness in our relationships with others and with the world. Basically, then, we need to be at peace with God and with ourselves before we can share peace with others. One of the most important tasks of Christians, which is to be peace-makers as distinct from being peace-breakers, becomes impossible if we are not at peace within ourselves.

If living peacefully includes living harmoniously and in unity, which is the sense Jesus intended, then we must humbly admit that our witness to peace and peaceful living is compromised seriously when we engage in conflict. We cannot honestly pray for peace in the world and remain indifferent to the discord that exists in our homes and workplaces. Such conflict needs to be resolved. At the heart of our prayer is our desire to strive for peace, the peace of Christ.

The presence of bitterness and resentment in our relationships and activities ensures that they are doomed to failure even before they begin. Therefore, we need to seek peace, which we can then share with other people.

For meditation

Do you suppose that I am here to bring peace on earth? No, I tell you, but rather division. (LUKE 12:51)

⊕
Twenty-First Sunday in Ordinary Time

GOSPEL READING: LUKE 13:22-30

REFLECTION

Sometimes Jesus seemed rather stern when he was teaching. For example, in response to the question, 'Sir, will there be only a few saved?', he replied: 'Try your best to enter by the narrow door, because, I tell you, many will try to enter and will not succeed' (Luke 13:23-24). This response must surely have shocked and disappointed many people who were listening to him. Jesus certainly did not pull any punches.

Basically, Jesus cautioned his listeners against being presumptuous about salvation. Salvation is ultimately about gaining entry to the kingdom of God and being in God's Blessed Presence for eternity. Significantly, unless people deliberately choose the kingdom and live in accordance with the teaching of Jesus, they will not automatically achieve salvation. Jesus said that to do this is to choose 'the narrow door' (Luke 13:24).

It is necessary to remind ourselves of this basic truth because, nowadays, there is a widespread presumption that all people will be saved. Some people argue that God loves us anyway, regardless of how we live, and that he will save us from the consequences of our sins and grant us eternal happiness – whether we want it or not.

But such an attitude denies that God has given us free will. If, in exercising our free will, we deliberately choose not to seek the kingdom of God, God will accept our choices and decisions, however reluctantly, and we will not gain entry to the kingdom. In the words of Jesus, we will not take our places with 'Abraham and Isaac and Jacob and all the prophets in the kingdom of God' (Luke 13:28). Similarly, we often have to accept that some people choose evil although we do not have to respect their choice.

We need to remember that Jesus' invitation to enter the kingdom is issued to everyone. However, it is not sufficient for us merely to desire the kingdom without agreeing to the challenge to change our lives so that they imitate Christ's life. There is no room for wishful thinking. The kingdom of God is far too important.

Entrance to the kingdom 'by the narrow door' is only possible for those who have made a serious commitment to preparing themselves for a life of intimate and eternal union with God in God's kingdom. This means undergoing conversion, turning away from sin and living in solidarity with Christ and his Church. In practice, this involves making correct choices in so many areas of life that conflict with modern permissiveness.

It will be useless to claim that we 'ate and drank' (Luke 13:27) with Jesus as we do spiritually with one another when we eat his Body and drink his Blood at celebrations of the Eucharist. Going to Mass in itself does not guarantee salvation unless it is accompanied by faithfulness to God's law, as taught by Christ and his Church, in our everyday relationships and routine activities.

Therefore, let us not be presumptuous about salvation. Instead, let us humbly ask God to be merciful to us sinners. While God's will is undoubtedly that everyone should be saved, the reality is that not all people will be saved. Adapting the popular motto to think globally while acting locally, let us live so that we will be among those who are saved, while praying and working for the salvation of all people. Moreover this is our prophetic vocation as baptised Christians.

For meditation

Men from east and west, from north and south, will
come to take their places at the feast in the kingdom
of God. (LUKE 13:29)

⊕
Twenty-Second Sunday in Ordinary Time

GOSPEL READING: LUKE 14:1, 7-14

REFLECTION

Most of us desire respect and status. We like to be
noticed and recognised by other people as being
important, and we often spend much time and effort
cultivating our reputations and seeking fame. Like
some guests at a wedding feast, we choose 'the place
of honour' (Luke 14:8). Yet Jesus said: 'For everyone
who exalts himself will be humbled, and the man who
humbles himself will be exalted' (Luke 14:11).

What did Jesus mean when he spoke these words?
He was effectively calling for the inversion of a well
established and long practiced custom. He was
emphasising the need to turn the reality of this world
on its head so that people would be ready for a new
and different reality in the kingdom of God.

Central to this new reality is an attitude of humility.
Humility is one of the main attributes of genuine
Christians. Jesus himself was always humble. There is
no place for arrogance or haughtiness in the Christian
life. Humility enables us to rise above our fallen human
nature so that our souls can be saved. In the parable of
the wedding feast, we are reminded that we will be
humbled if we have exalted ourselves and that we will
be exalted if we have humbled ourselves.

Jesus' message is simple: the greater we are in worldly terms, the more humble we must become. For example, when invited to be guests at a celebration, we take the lowest places at table. In other words, we need to learn to be lowly and let God invite us to where God wishes us to be, just as the host at a party may invite us up higher.

Humility, or lowliness, is a virtue and, like all virtues, needs to be nurtured. It demands much effort and willpower because it requires that we 'go against the grain' by becoming selfless and putting other people and their needs before our own. An attitude of humility teaches us that God's law is to be obeyed at all times, especially when there is a tendency nowadays to behave as we choose. Conforming to God's will requires much humility. Developing an attitude of humility is a major part of the ongoing conversion which is so central to Christianity.

Obviously, Jesus did not recommend an attitude of humility as a deceitful way to get invited to the top table. Rather, he taught that an attitude of humility characterises people who know that their importance is determined not in earthly terms but in the knowledge that they are loved by God who saves them from sin through Christ's suffering and death.

None of us likes those who are conceited and self-centred. Similarly, other people will not like us if we lack humility and are arrogant. Arrogance debilitates us and prevents us from achieving our full spiritual potential. Thus we need to put ourselves last if we wish to be great in God's sight.

Are we humble? Do we seek power and privilege and prestige? If the answer to these questions is 'Yes', we need to remember the words of Jesus: 'Everyone who exalts himself will be humbled, and the man who humbles himself will be exalted' (Luke 14:11).

For meditation
Everyone who exalts himself will be humbled, and the man who humbles himself will be exalted.
(LUKE 14:11)

⊕
Twenty-Third Sunday in Ordinary Time

GOSPEL READING: LUKE 14:25-33

REFLECTION

Being a disciple of Jesus is not easy. It demands total commitment and much self-discipline, so much so that it sometimes seems impossible. Indeed it is not an exaggeration to say that there is often a heavy price to be paid for discipleship, especially regarding family members and personal possessions.

Jesus was absolutely unequivocal about this when he said: 'If any man comes to me without hating his father, mother, wife, children, brothers, sisters, yes and his own life too, he cannot be my disciple' (Luke 14:26). But Jesus did not stop there. He also said: 'Anyone who does not carry his cross and come after me cannot be my disciple' (Luke 14:27) and 'None of you can be my disciple unless he gives up all his possessions' (Luke 14:33).

Jesus does not intend us to interpret literally his words about family relationships and possessions. He does not want us to 'hate' anyone, least of all our families. But he was deliberately exaggerating so that his message would be understood by his listeners. His message is clear, however. We must put God first. We must put the truth first. Even our families do not come before God in our lives. That is what Jesus meant.

Basically, then, there are three requirements if we want to be Jesus' disciples. Firstly, we are obliged to prioritise our relationships so that our commitment to Jesus comes before our commitments to everyone else. We cannot use the excuse that our family duties come before God's law because Jesus has told us that this is not the case. God is always first.

Secondly, we are expected to engage in self-denial by allowing whatever suffering we cannot alleviate to transform us from being selfish to being selfless, and putting the needs of others before our own needs. (This is what it means to carry our cross every day.) We are all required to share in the cross, and by his suffering and death on the cross Jesus has shown us that suffering can have immense value in the eyes of God.

Thirdly, it is necessary that we do not become attached to our material possessions because, from the perspective of the Good News, they are means to an end instead of an end in themselves. We are expected to trust in God's providence and not gather up material goods because this kind of acquisitiveness makes us become more and more attached to this world and less receptive to the spiritual riches that we require to enable us to prepare for the next world.

The message is unambiguous: Jesus demands total commitment from us. This does not mean, of course, that we cannot be interested in other people and things. But our priority must be our relationship with him. There can be no half measure. This is the cost of true discipleship.

For meditation
None of you can be my disciple unless he gives up all his possessions. (LUKE 14:33)

⊕
Twenty-Fourth Sunday in Ordinary Time

GOSPEL READING: LUKE 15:1-32

REFLECTION

The parable of the prodigal son has sometimes been described as the most perfect piece of literature ever written. It is certainly one of the most moving stories used by Jesus to teach us about God's nature and our own fallen human nature, and is one of the most famous parables recorded in the New Testament.

This story is familiar: two sons, who appear to be quite different in personality and character, and a loving father. The younger son wants his inheritance and independence. His father agrees, sadly no doubt, just like many parents today. Unfortunately, the son loses everything and realises that his independence has turned to loneliness. He returns home, having come to his senses, and admits his guilt: 'Father, I have sinned against heaven and against you. I no longer deserve to be called your son' (Luke 15:21).

The elder son protests against his father's decision to celebrate the younger son's return home. According to Jesus' teaching in the parable, God is like a generous and loving father who welcomes home his son without hesitation. All that matters is that his younger son is home, has admitted his foolishness and confessed his wrongdoing, and expressed his desire to make reparation for his sins.

Notice that these steps are similar to those taken when celebrating the sacrament of reconciliation: we confess our sins, express our sorrow and seek to repair the damage caused. As the father responded to his errant son, by throwing his arms around him and inviting everyone to celebrate, so God responds lovingly to the requests of sinners. And for the same reason: because this sinner 'was dead and has come to life; he was lost and is found' (Luke 15:32).

The parable of the prodigal son and his loving father has the potential to change us, if we learn from it, because it identifies precisely the weakness in our human nature. There are traits of us in both sons. Like the younger son, we try to live independently, often ignoring God and the path to holiness. Yet experience teaches us that such selfishness leads to unhappiness.

We are sometimes like the elder son, the faithful one trying to live a holy life but, perhaps, feeling that others who are less concerned about the things of God do very well out of life anyway and are more appreciated than ourselves. But using the parable, Jesus teaches us to focus only on what is right. Thus it was correct that the younger son should admit his guilt, recognise his father's love for him and resolve to respect and love him in the future. It was also proper that the elder son was a faithful, conscientious son throughout his life.

At the end of the parable, we are not told whether the elder son attended the banquet held in honour of his errant brother, but we know that the father desired that his elder son welcome his brother, putting aside all resentment. It is an invitation to all faithful Christians to imitate God's love and forgiveness in our families and in the wider community.

For meditation

While he was still a long way off, his father saw him and was moved with pity. (LUKE 15:20)

SEE THE FOURTH SUNDAY OF LENT FOR ANOTHER REFLECTION ON THE PARABLE OF THE PRODIGAL SON.

⊕
Twenty-Fifth Sunday in Ordinary Time

GOSPEL READING: LUKE 16:1-13

REFLECTION

One of the most challenging teachings of Jesus is summarised in the phrase: 'You cannot be the slave both of God and of money' (Luke 16:13). A similar phrase states: 'If then you cannot be trusted with money, that tainted thing, who will trust you with genuine riches?' (Luke 16:11). Note that money is 'tainted' because we have to work for it; earning our living by the sweat of our brow is a result of the sin of disobedience (see Genesis 3).

No surprise, then, that Jesus contrasts God with money. What is the significant difference between God and money? In effect, God and genuine riches (which are not the riches of this world) are spiritual realities whereas money is a material reality tainted by sin. The lesson is simple. It is the spiritual dimensions of life that matter more than the material dimensions. We are challenged to prioritise our lives so that God is always first.

As a result of our fallen world and fallen human nature, we need money to live. But we are forbidden by Jesus to become attached to money and all that it can buy. Divine Providence provides all that we need to live unless, of course, we are somehow deprived because of other people's greed. Thus we may earn and use money but it is always of less importance to us than God and the spiritual riches he gives us through Christ and his Church.

The earth and its produce are given to us by God so that we can use them while we prepare for the next life.

If material possessions become more important than anything or anyone else in our lives, we run the risk of losing eternal life with God because they lead us away from God by convincing us that we are autonomous and self-sufficient with no need to rely on God. Instead of being in control of our money and other possessions, then, they control us.

The opposite of such an approach to living is to realise that all our possessions, including our time and talents, derive from God. We dedicate them to God by doing his will in our lives. We learn to recognise, like all genuine Christian disciples, that we, like Christ, are in this world but not of it.

Does this mean that we cannot have money and that we should be poor? No, but we must use our money and other resources properly, being prepared to share them with those who are in greater need than us. Money is meant to be used to make the quality of life better for ourselves and other people. Actually, our true wealth is not to be found in what we keep but in what we freely give away.

Business people especially need to remember this. If profit becomes more important than our employees and our customers, we exploit them and use them only for our own selfish gain. Similarly, workers must not demand unjust pay increases which may price the business out of the marketplace. Greed takes different forms and we must be alert to this, always seeking to reflect Christian values in the workplace.

All of Christ's teaching is about faithfulness to God's law. Using different parables and sayings, Jesus traces the spiritual path that we faithfully walk if we wish to save our souls. In this instance, he is teaching us that, to be faithful to God, to keep on the spiritual path desired for us by God, we do not allow 'tainted' money to replace God and the genuine riches of our faith.

Which is first in our lives: God or money?

For meditation

You cannot be the slave both of God and of money.
(LUKE 16:13)

⊕
Twenty-Sixth Sunday in Ordinary Time

GOSPEL READING: LUKE 16:19-31

REFLECTION

We often mistakenly assume that we sin by what we think and say and do, whenever our actions are not in accordance with God's commandments. We think that our only sins are what may be described as sins of commission. However, in reality, as the parable of the rich man and Lazarus teaches us, we can also have sins of omission. In other words, we can sometimes sin by what we do NOT think and NOT say and NOT do.

Such was the situation of the rich man in the parable. While he was alive, he enjoyed a good life. He dressed in beautiful clothes and he feasted magnificently every day. The parable does not suggest that he lived badly or that he behaved despicably, although he was always oblivious to the poor man at his gate.

Later, when the rich man died and was tormented in Hades, he discovered that his most serious sins were sins of omission. Abraham told him: 'Remember that during your life good things came your way, just as bad things came the way of Lazarus. Now he is being comforted here while you are in agony' (Luke 16:25).

The rich man, because of his indifference, had failed to notice Lazarus at his gate and had not responded with kindness and compassion.

In not reaching out to Lazarus, even if his indifference was apparently unintentional, the rich man sinned because he ignored another human being who was in need. Regarding human laws, ignorance is no defence. For example, we are held responsible for breaking traffic laws even if we are unaware of them. God's law is written in our hearts and the Natural Law (that is, law based on the natural order which has universal application) is clear: we must help others in need, irrespective of race, status or money. So there is no legitimate excuse for inaction.

The story of the rich man could easily be the story of any one of us. There are so many people who never seem to commit any infringements of God's law. They never assault others physically or verbally. They never steal from work or tell lies about their friends. They say their prayers and go to church.

Nonetheless, they omit much of what God desires by not noticing the plights of other people and not defending the truth. It has often been said that all that is necessary for evil to succeed is for good people to say and do nothing. For Christians, it is not enough to say nothing or to do nothing. Indifference and complacency are two of the most insidious and damaging sins of omission.

The lesson from the parable of the rich man and Lazarus is clear. Whenever we examine our consciences, it is not sufficient to focus only on what we have thought and said and done. We also need to focus on our omissions, what we have not thought and not said and not done, because they could be far more serious and sinful.

Do we watch for those who are poor in so many different ways, spiritually and morally, around us? Are we like the rich man who passes by obliviously or do we stop and reach out a helping hand? To be a true Christian disciple, we are obliged to be attentive to the cry of the poor.

For meditation
Good things came your way, just as bad things came the way of Lazarus. Now he is being comforted here while you are in agony. (LUKE 16:25)

⊕
Twenty-Seventh Sunday in Ordinary Time

GOSPEL READING: LUKE 17:5-19

REFLECTION

Even a little faith can accomplish much. Jesus taught his disciples that, if their faith was the size of a mustard seed, they could say to a mulberry tree: 'Be uprooted and planted in the sea' (Luke 17:6), and it would obey them. Yet he wondered if he would find any faith at all when he returned to the earth. And so we might well ask: how great is our faith?

Significantly, when Jesus preached he invited people to be faith-filled people. He challenged them to let their faith influence their attitudes and actions. He reminded them that the fundamental requirement of faith is a complete openness to God. Jesus challenges each of us in the same way.

It seems self-evident to say that faith is absolutely necessary for the Christian life. Without an active faith there is no Christian life. Faith is both a gift from God and a human response to God. It enables us to see beyond the ordinary events of life. It is an inner power that helps us to discover and believe in a caring God who is always present and active in our lives and in the world. It enables us to trust God completely, regardless of the circumstances in which we find ourselves.

Faith is essentially a gift from God by which we freely accept God's self-revelation (that is, self-disclosure) in Christ. It is always a free gift that can either be accepted or rejected. God does not impose the gift of faith on anyone. Basically, faith is a relationship between two persons – God and the individual human being. Therefore, it can never be the result of human reasoning alone. There has to be some awareness of a personal relationship being formed and maintained between God and the human being.

Not surprisingly, then, faith deals with the questions of ultimate meaning in life, questions about origin, purpose and destiny. Our faith saves us because it teaches us that our eternal destiny is to be with God and we spend our lives searching for that destiny. In the words of St Augustine referring to God, 'Our hearts are restless until they rest in Thee'. So faith in God is a free, reasonable and personal response to God's self-revelation. God initiates this self-revelation and invites us to respond through faith leading to personal knowledge and commitment and also to share in the life of salvation that is offered to us.

When we read the Bible, we quickly discover that faith as an expression of the relationship between God and us becomes the 'way of life' for those who are on the way to salvation. Faith is continually maturing, like all genuine relationships. Otherwise it dies. It cannot remain the same. For Christians, faith is the acceptance of the person and saving message of Jesus Christ. The sign or proof of such acceptance is repentance and conversion to a way of life that is deeply rooted in the Good News.

How great is our faith? How much do we trust God? The answer is to be found in our fidelity to his commandments and the teaching of the Church. In these times when many people claim that belief in God is irrelevant, it is necessary that we pray for a deeper faith, a faith that sustains us in our relationship with God and seeks to win many souls for Christ.

For meditation
Increase our faith. (LUKE 17:5)

⊕
Twenty-Eighth Sunday in Ordinary Time

GOSPEL READING: LUKE 17:5-19

REFLECTION

During Jesus' lifetime, lepers were segregated from other people and excluded from society. They were to be clearly recognisable so that they could be avoided. They were banished to the margins of society, stripped of their dignity and shunned. Lepers were rejected and dejected people.

In contrast, Jesus adopted an inclusive approach. He refused to turn away the ten lepers who approached him. He wanted to cure them and he did so. Jesus certainly treated them differently from the way other people treated them. In doing so, he focused his attention on those who were on the margins of the crowd gathered around him, inviting them to assume a centre-stage role, much to the annoyance of the other people who were present. Regrettably, however, only one of the ten cured lepers displayed his gratitude to Jesus.

Gratitude is an essential ingredient of the Christian life. This was emphasised by Jesus when he expressed in surprise: 'Were not all ten made clean? The other nine, where are they?' (Luke 17:17). But notice the reason for Jesus' surprise. It was not for the same reason that most of us dislike ingratitude. If we give something away, a gift for example, or if we offer to help friends or neighbours, we expect them to appreciate our thoughtfulness, our time, our money, or whatever it is we have given. Certainly, if we had the power to heal someone's illness, we would expect that person to show gratitude.

But Jesus tells us why he is surprised that nine of the lepers cured by him did not return to give thanks. 'It seems that no one has come back to give praise to God, except this foreigner' (Luke 17:18). This is significant. By being grateful, we are recognising God as the author of all gifts.

Jesus challenges us to stop treating people as lepers. He invites us to be compassionate and kind when we meet people who are suffering, especially those whose suffering causes them to be shunned by society so that we may facilitate the process of healing and the restoration of wholeness in the lives of broken and shattered people. It can be as simple as a welcoming smile, an encouraging word, a loving gesture – anything that gives an otherwise dejected person a renewed sense of dignity and self-worth. It may also be as risky as giving someone a second chance when no one else will do the same or forgiving someone who has hurt us deeply.

However, Jesus also challenges us to be grateful because by our gratitude we glorify and praise God, who is the giver of life. That is the basis of the Christian life.

For meditation

No one has come back to give praise to God,
except this foreigner. (LUKE 17:18)

⊕
Twenty-Ninth Sunday in Ordinary Time

GOSPEL READING: LUKE 18:1-8

REFLECTION

Jesus' parable of the corrupt judge and the persistent widow is a parable about prayer. More specifically, it deals with perseverance in prayer. The basic lesson is that we need to pray continually and never lose heart by remaining confident that God always listens and answers.

Prayer is communication with God. It is an expression of the relationship that exists between God and us, both individually and collectively. Communication involves listening as well as speaking, and genuine listening requires that we are prepared to change if necessary. This is how our relationship with God deepens. If we do not listen to God – and God has so much to say to us – we cannot claim to be praying sincerely.

Sometimes we think that God does not respond to our prayer of intercession. We presume that, if our prayer is not answered as we would wish, God has ignored us. It may seem that God is indifferent and disinterested. But this is untrue. 'Yes' is not the only answer to prayer. Does it ever occur to us that God may say 'No'? What if our request is not in accordance with God's will? Surely God is unlikely to act against his plan.

Many people think that prayer is a magic formula like 'abracadabra!' If God does not wish to do what these people ask, they doubt his existence. For example, in the past some people have expressed dismay that God did not answer their prayer for the safe release of hostages captured by terrorists. Certainly, we are encouraged to pray that God's grace will touch the hearts of hardened sinners and we can be sure that God's grace is as readily available to those terrorists as it is to us.

That the terrorists refuse to be influenced by God's grace is a result of human sinfulness, not God's refusal to listen to and answer people's prayer. Their dismay rightly deserves to be directed wholly at the terrorists. God has indeed answered their prayer. No prayer is ever wasted.

What is critical, however, is that, like the widow in the parable, we persevere so that we can discern why God answers our prayer in the way that he does. Significantly, the parable does not compare God to the corrupt judge. Instead it focuses on the widow's persistence. Her persistence eventually wins the day. Furthermore, even if an unjust judge occasionally does what is correct, how much more will God (who loved the world so much that he sent his only Son) respond and help us?

How persistent are we when we pray? Do we persevere like the widow in the parable? The widow is a model for our prayer because she recognised her need for help. More importantly, she believed that there was someone listening who could and would help her. Jesus challenged his disciples to imitate the persistent widow by praying continually and never losing heart.

Jesus spent much of his time praying and he encouraged his disciples to do the same. Prayer prepares us to deal effectively with the various challenges of life. It is the most significant activity in our lives. If we do not pray, we will never understand God's will.

The challenge of the parable of the corrupt judge and the persistent widow is to persevere in prayer, especially when it seems to be unanswered. Remember, prayer is always answered because God never stops listening to us and caring for us. We need to become more trusting.

For meditation
Will not God see justice done to his chosen who cry to him day and night even when he delays to help them? (LUKE 18:7)

⊕
Thirtieth Sunday in Ordinary Time

GOSPEL READING: LUKE 18:9-14

REFLECTION

The parable of the Pharisee and the tax collector at prayer, like Jesus' other parables, had a surprising ending. During his prayer in the Temple, the Pharisee, who seemingly was a paragon of virtue, thanked God that he was not grasping, unjust and adulterous. He was especially grateful that he was not like the tax collector who was also present. Yet the Pharisee did not leave the Temple 'at rights with God' (Luke 18:14) because he was arrogant and judgemental when he prayed.

The lesson is obvious: there is no place for arrogance in our prayer. We need to be humble in God's presence. Otherwise, we are wasting our time when we pray.

In contrast to the Pharisee, the tax collector, a relatively unpopular official in society, demonstrated an attitude of humility during his prayer. He said very simply: 'God, be merciful to me, a sinner' (Luke 18:13). His humility ensured that he departed 'at rights with God'.

When he finished telling the parable, Jesus summarised his teaching by saying that 'everyone who exalts himself will be humbled, but the man who humbles himself will be exalted' (Luke 18:14). Once again, Jesus turned the conventional presumptions about Pharisees and tax collectors upside down. This had particular relevance for his listeners because they were 'people who prided themselves on being virtuous and despised everyone else' (Luke 18:9). Is it any wonder that Jesus was detested by the Pharisees and scribes?

What, then, are the main characteristics of humble Christian disciples? Firstly, they realise that they are not the most important people and that God must always be first. Secondly, they do not allow themselves to be fooled by a false sense of self-importance and they treat others as they would like others to treat them. In addition, they are not quick to judge others and are appreciative of the love and forgiveness that God generously shares with them.

Humble people recognise that they are imperfect. With faith they pray for God's strength to help them improve each day. They are aware of their sinfulness and they know that they cannot change their lives fundamentally without God's grace. They come into God's presence with no pretence.

Regrettably, arrogant people destroy many of the opportunities that God gives them to change for the better. They assume that they can do everything themselves without any help. They may even think that there is no need for God. They judge others hastily – as distinct from speaking the truth prophetically – and rejoice in their downfall. The Pharisee was displeasing to God because he compared himself favourably to the tax collector instead of acknowledging that he, too, was a sinner. Arrogant people focus on external appearances when interiority is what matters.

The truth, of course, is that we should all be so busy trying to imitate God's goodness that we do not have time to judge other people. If we are engaged doing the Lord's work, then we will not have time to be distracted by lack of humility, a much undervalued virtue today.

Being humble involves reliance on God and trust in God's loving mercy. It means being honest with ourselves about the state of our own souls. How reliant on God are we? When we pray, do we present our true selves to God or do we pretend that we are someone else? The parable of the Pharisee and the tax collector at prayer invites us to examine the attitudes that motivate our prayer. Let our prayer always be: 'God, be merciful to me, a sinner' (Luke 18:13).

For meditation
This man went home again at rights with God; the other did not. (LUKE 18:14)

⊕
Thirty-First Sunday in Ordinary Time

GOSPEL READING: LUKE 19:1-10

REFLECTION
How anxious are we to see Jesus? How much do we want to be in his presence? Do we search every day to discover the presence of Jesus around us and, in doing so, do we realise that Jesus is also searching for us?

Zacchaeus was so anxious to see what kind of man Jesus was that he climbed a sycamore tree in order to be able to see Jesus passing by. Zacchaeus had obviously heard about Jesus before. He was intrigued and he wanted to know Jesus. But Zacchaeus was a small person and he could easily have been lost in the crowd. Also, being a tax collector, he was unpopular with people and shunned by them. Yet he was determined to see Jesus. Nobody, regardless of size and importance, was going to prevent him. As he waited for Jesus, Jesus searched for him, found him and brought salvation into his life. Jesus offers to do the same for all of us.

Sometimes other people make us feel small and insignificant. We allow them to diminish our self-esteem. We may feel alienated. At times, too, we may think that God has deserted us. It is as if we are outcasts and we begin to wallow in self-pity. However, the story about Zacchaeus challenges us never to let this happen. Zacchaeus did not permit alienation and scorn to deflect him from what he desired. He wanted to be near Jesus and Jesus more than fulfilled his wish.

Significantly, there is no record of Zacchaeus responding negatively to the people who treated him badly. He readily acknowledged his failures and imperfections. He was truly humble.

If only all of us could be more like Zacchaeus after his encounter with Jesus. We need not be apologetic in our quest for Jesus. Like Zacchaeus, we grasp the opportunities for salvation that are offered to us by Christ. We gain nothing if we collapse when other people exclude us and treat us badly. They often do so but we cannot allow them to diminish our dignity and undermine our self-confidence by placing unnecessary obstacles in our way.

Several years ago, I knew a student who was dyslexic. Although he was often treated insensitively by some of his teachers and fellow students, he never allowed other people to shatter his self-confidence or to make him feel unimportant. He was like Zacchaeus. He knew what he wanted from life and he set about achieving it gently but firmly. He went to university and is now an excellent teacher.

Like Zacchaeus, most of us would eagerly go to meet Jesus if we were told that he was arriving in our town or village. Yet we know that he is present in our lives and world already. He is most especially present in the Eucharist which is celebrated and reserved in our churches. Thus we do not have to travel far to meet him!

What are we prepared to do in order to be in Jesus' presence? How far are we prepared to go to gain salvation? Zacchaeus took a risk and the risk was worth taking. Not alone did he meet Jesus, but Jesus changed his life completely. Jesus will do the same for us if we permit him to find us while we search for him.

For meditation

The Son of Man has come to seek out and save what was lost. (Luke 19:10)

⊕

Thirty-Second Sunday in Ordinary Time

Gospel reading: Luke 20:27-38

Reflection

Some people argue that there is no life after death and that, therefore, only this life matters. Consequently, they live without any reference to what is beyond this life because, as far as they are concerned, death is the end. Of those people who believe in the afterlife, some claim that the afterlife is all-important and, for them, what happens in this life has no long-term significance because, ultimately, it is only life after death that matters. They do not perceive a link between this life and the next life.

Yet it is clear from the Bible that belief in the resurrection of the dead is central to the lives of many people. Jesus teaches his disciples about the resurrection of the dead. He corrects the Sadducees' speculation that all relationships in the next life are the same as in this life: 'The children of this world take wives and husbands, but those who are judged worthy of a place in the other world and in the resurrection from the dead do not marry because they can no longer die, for they are the same as the angels' (Luke 20:34-36). Life after death is radically new and different from life on earth.

Jesus Christ is living proof of life after death, and Christians believe that all people will rise from the dead as he rose from the dead. The resurrection of the dead is pivotal to Jesus' teaching because he died and rose from the dead so that all people would share in his death and resurrection and gain eternal life. He has taught us that, even if we die, we always live in him. That is why Jesus argued that God 'is God, not of the dead, but of the living' (Luke 20:38).

But Christians also believe that there is a definite connection between human life in this world and life after death. The two are inextricably linked because we can only enter the next life by dying in this life. It is during our earthly lives that we learn to know God who invites us to journey through death to our true home in heaven.

How we live in this world has a bearing on the next life. We cannot be with God forever in heaven unless we are with God during life here on earth. The best way, indeed the only way, to prepare for the next life is to live this life as fully as possible in the presence of God. We do this by being faithful to Christ's teaching and example.

The new, radiant life that Jesus experienced after he rose from the dead was the result of the truly human and hope-filled life he lived before his death. So there is a connection between life on this earth and the afterlife. Both form a continuum. Like Jesus, we are called to live as fully and humanly as possible in this world so that after death we can enjoy God's heavenly presence forever.

For meditation

He is God, not of the dead, but of the living.
(LUKE 20:38)

⊕
Thirty-Third Sunday in Ordinary Time

GOSPEL READING: LUKE 21:5-19

REFLECTION

Sometimes the word of God presents stories of destruction, desolation and fear. Evil-doers will be burned. Everything will be destroyed. Nations will engage in battle. There will be earthquakes, plagues and famines. These stories are all the more frightening in the aftermath of the appalling terrorist events that regularly happen in our world.

These stories in the Bible are usually interpreted as referring to the end of the world and to the final judgement. People who live evil and arrogant lives will pay a heavy price. In the end they will be punished for their wickedness and wrongdoing towards other people. Therefore, all of us are warned about the consequences of being ruthless and unscrupulous in this life. How we live in the present will determine how we will be judged at the end of time. We will have to accept responsibility for our behaviour in this world.

But these stories may also be interpreted as referring to the personal catastrophes that can affect any one of us as we struggle with life. Our whole world can be shattered for any number of reasons. Perhaps our spouse or one of our children dies tragically. Maybe we become redundant from work with no possibility of further employment for the remainder of our working lives. In such situations we can begin to think that our world and our lives have ended.

Whether the disaster is the end of the world or a devastating personal catastrophe, the instinctive reaction is to become despondent and to abandon hope. After all, there seems to be no worthwhile future. Nothing has meaning anymore. Nobody cares. But the word of God, in addition to its warnings about destruction and desolation, also offers us hope. We are invited to trust in God when circumstances and situations are desperate.

Jesus teaches us that, even when we are betrayed and hated by other people because of our commitment to him, not even a hair of our heads will be lost and our endurance will save us. In the midst of chaos and annihilation there is hope because we can always trust God. God is truly present, in good times and bad times. We are reminded that God is in those around us by the many small and large ways in which individual people and countries respond generously and unstintingly to natural catastrophes. Countless acts of kindness, generosity and communion often emerge out of catastrophes.

A question for us as we reflect on the word of God is: do we trust God even in desperate situations? If we do, then we will remain hopeful and confident that, whatever people say and do, we will be with God forever.

For meditation

Your endurance will win you your lives. (LUKE 21:19)

⊕
Our Lord Jesus Christ, Universal King

GOSPEL READING: LUKE 23:35-43

REFLECTION

On the last Sunday of the liturgical year, we acknowledge Jesus Christ as our Lord and Universal King. Many of us have difficulty with the notions of king and kingship and kingdom. They seem to be increasingly incompatible with the principle of democracy that typically describes how our society is organised. Where kings exist in our world, they are frequently criticised about luxurious and wild lifestyles. They are certainly not described as servants of their people.

The image we have of Jesus does not resemble a king when we reflect on his simple lifestyle and listen to the account of him hanging on a cross dying as a common criminal. Our image of a king is someone who is majestic and sovereign, not someone who dies in such a humiliating and shameful way. It is such a contradiction in terms. Yet we refer to Jesus Christ as our King who came to serve rather than to be served. He is the one who preached that the kingdom of God was very near and who enabled people to glimpse it through his miracles.

How do we understand Christ to be our King? He turns the notion of king on its head. He is a servant king. He is not a king who lords it over his subjects and exploits them. But Jesus goes even further than serving his people. He saves them by dying for them.

The cross becomes Jesus' throne and his crowning in glory. There are many contradictions in how Jesus is treated at the end of his life. The crowds greet him like a king on Palm Sunday. A few days later, the same people demand that he be crucified. They accuse him of being a king and they treat him like a criminal. He is dressed in a royal cloak and he is crowned with thorns. He dies a cruel and shameful death. There is no state funeral for him.

It is often observed that today's society is a fickle society where celebrities are 'here today and gone tomorrow'. As we know, human beings are often whimsical and compulsive. By stark contrast, God is loyal, steadfast and dependable. Fortunately, God's love for us is not dependant on our positive response to him. God's love for us in Christ is unfaltering. We, along with all the other generations of people in history, are his people. Jesus died because of our sins. He brought us life on the cross even though he lost his own life there. He proved that God's love for us is never-ending.

The Feast of Christ the King is a fitting celebration for the end of the Church's year. We affirm our belief in God who rules us in love rather than power. We acknowledge the mercy and forgiveness of God who teaches us through the compassion of his Son on the cross that, like the repentant criminal, our true home is in paradise.

For meditation
Jesus, remember me when you come into your kingdom. (LUKE 23:42)

HOLY DAYS AND ⊕
SOME OTHER FEASTS

⊕
2 February: The Presentation of the Lord

GOSPEL READING: LUKE 2:22-40

REFLECTION

Traditionally, and quite rightly, the Church has always believed that Mary and Joseph were exemplary parents. As we would expect, their priorities were correct. Shortly after Jesus' birth, for example, they brought him to the Temple and presented him to the Lord, as part of the ritual of their Jewish faith. They consecrated him to God, thereby acknowledging that he had come from God. Thus they recognised that their task of rearing him was a sacred task.

However, their parental task was not complete when they dedicated Jesus in the Temple. In fact, it was only beginning. Subsequently, they spent much time rearing him and teaching him by their own faith and good example so that, in later years, he would appreciate the importance of faith and religious practice in daily life.

In most cases, parents are our first teachers and, normally, they are our best teachers. Although Jesus was God's Son in a different way from how other human beings are God's sons and daughters (Jesus is fully human, yet he is also divine), he still experienced parental influence as he matured.

All parents have a similar task to Mary and Joseph. Their children's lives begin in God and parents have both the privilege and the responsibility of rearing their children conscious of this most fundamental truth. Being a parent is an onerous undertaking. Parents often have to forego their own plans in the interest of their children's wellbeing. They need to review their priorities continually so that their children will learn that God is to be at the centre of their lives.

Unfortunately, some parents do not exercise their God-given duty to safeguard their children's interests. For example, how many parents fail to monitor their children's Internet access or what they watch on television? Or how many parents make a serious effort to ensure that their children's friends do not lead them away from living in accordance with the Good News?

The Christian faith is shared from one generation to the next when parents and children remember their consecration to God. The task demands commitment and selflessness from parents. The faith is taught by both word and example. This means that parents cannot simply teach Christianity to their children as they might teach grammar and mathematics. Christian faith is very practical and can only be transmitted successfully by parents through daily examples of Christian living. Otherwise, Christianity remains just another theory instead of becoming a challenging, yet fulfilling, way of living.

If the family home is not characterised by forbearance, gentleness and forgiveness, children will not appreciate how necessary these virtues are for wholesome living. If parents and children do not pray together, an essential element of communication with God will be missing from children's lives. A prayerful way of living must be learned through practice and parents need to lead by example.

We were consecrated to God shortly after we were born and baptism is the sign of our consecration. Do we remember that our lives are dedicated to God? And are we grateful to our parents for the sacrifices they made as they shared their faith and as they tried to teach us how to live as children consecrated to God?

For meditation

You see this child: he is destined for the fall and for the rising of many in Israel, destined to be a sign that is rejected. (LUKE 2:34)

⊕
15 August: The Assumption of the Blessed Virgin Mary

GOSPEL READING (MASS DURING THE DAY): LUKE 1:39-56

REFLECTION

The Feast of the Assumption, one of Mary's principal feasts, has been observed since the seventh century. It celebrates the Church's belief that, at the end of her earthly life, the sinless Blessed Virgin Mary, who is the Mother of Jesus, was taken body and soul into heavenly glory. Thus her body did not corrupt in the grave or tomb. This belief was defined as a dogma of faith by Pope Pius XII in 1950.

Significantly, there is a notable difference between Mary's assumption into heaven and Jesus' ascension to heaven. Jesus ascended to heaven by his own power because he was both divine and human. In contrast, Mary was assumed into heaven not by her own will but by God's will. Her assumption anticipated the resurrection from the dead which will happen for everyone else, although not everyone will necessarily go to heaven.

The importance of the Feast of the Assumption is that it is a reminder that heaven exists. Heaven awaits us if we live in accordance with the teaching of Christ and his Church. Mary's assumption into heaven is significant for our Catholic faith because it is the natural conclusion of her saying 'Yes' to the angel Gabriel when asked to cooperate with God's plan for salvation by becoming the Mother of God's Son.

Mary's assumption was, in a sense, the logical end to her earthly life. The Feast draws our attention to the fact that, what God has done for Mary, he also desires to do for each one of us. However, unlike Mary, we will not be assumed body and soul into heaven. Instead, our bodies will be buried and they will decay until the resurrection of the dead on the Last Day.

When we celebrate the Feast, we have an opportunity to focus on where we are called to be. We are encouraged because we know that one human being, other than Jesus, is already where the remainder of us pray and hope to be for eternity. But we cannot presume that we will automatically attain the gift of heaven. Our destiny depends on how we live in this life. Increasingly, many people assume that, after death, they will be in heaven regardless of how they live during this life.

Mary is in heaven now because, after being conceived without Original Sin, she said 'Yes' to God throughout her entire earthly life and, with the help of God's grace, remained sinless. While we will not be taken to heaven in the same way as Mary, the result can be the same if we, like Mary, continue to say 'Yes' to God and are always open to his will. What is different is that Mary is there sooner than us. Furthermore, she enjoys a uniquely privileged position as Queen of Heaven where she intercedes powerfully for us.

As Catholics, we need to cultivate a special devotion to Mary. For example, whenever we pray the Rosary we are effectively walking with Mary through the life of Jesus. The Feast of the Assumption offers us a chance to renew our faith and to rededicate our efforts to be faithful to God's plan for our daily lives. It challenges us to turn away from sin and to imitate Mary who was always faithful to God. It gives us hope for eternity whereby we thank God for Mary's life and faith.

For meditation

The Almighty has done great things for me and exalted the lowly. (LUKE 1:49, 52)

⊕
14 September: The Triumph of the Cross

GOSPEL READING: JOHN 3:13-17

REFLECTION

Fundamental to Jesus' preaching was his teaching about the undeniable link between death and being raised from the dead. His reference to death was not only to physical death but also death to a sinful life.

Jesus taught that anyone wishing to become his disciple would have to take up his or her cross and follow him. Many people were impressed by his teaching and would have liked to join him and his disciples. But they could not because they were unwilling to embrace the Cross in their daily lives.

In one sense, it is understandable that people would avoid the Cross because it brings pain and discomfort. It requires humility and being different from the often sinful options chosen by the majority of people. Yet, in another sense, the Cross cannot be avoided because it teaches us that we need to lose our life every day in order to save it, abandoning sin so that we may gain eternal happiness.

The Cross takes many forms. It is suffering and illness for some people. For others, it is rejection and persecution because they are faithful to the truth and reject the false values and spiritual blindness around them. Embracing the Cross is necessary for the Christian disciple. The essential teaching of Jesus is summarised in his words: 'If anyone wants to be a follower of mine, let him renounce himself and take up his cross every day and follow me' (Luke 9:23). Certainly, it is not by our own strength but by God's grace that we are able to carry our crosses.

The Cross is the major Christian symbol. It symbolises the paradoxical journey from weakness to strength, from defeat to victory, and from rejection to acceptance. Thus the Cross is at the heart of our Christian faith. It reminds us of God's endless mercy and of Jesus' self-giving to save us from the consequences of our sins. There can be no life without death, especially death to selfishness and other sins. The constant challenge for Christians is to understand that there can be no Resurrection without firstly undergoing death on the Cross. There can be no Easter Sunday without Good Friday.

We are invited to accept the Cross in life's small inconveniences and everyday decisions as well as in life's dreadful tragedies. Sometimes people who have not experienced great bereavement or suffered from serious illness erroneously assume that the Cross does not impinge on their lives. In reality, the Cross visits everyone at some stage through ill health, the death of those who are close to us, or in the various difficulties and disagreements with other people, and in the worries and anxieties of daily living. Suffering and unhappiness are transformed by Christ's suffering, resulting in God's glorification and our liberation.

Accepting the Cross becomes a normal part of life for Christians. The Cross calls us to total commitment, even to laying down our lives for the salvation of our souls and those of others.

True conversion occurs when we learn to put other people before ourselves and when we accept God's will, especially when we would prefer to ignore it. The questions we need to ask include: where is the Cross in our lives? Are we dying to sin every day so that we will gain eternal life? Embracing our daily crosses is the essence of holiness and the sign of true discipleship.

On the Feast of the Triumph of the Cross, it is appropriate to pray: Lord Jesus, I give you my hands to do your work. I give you my feet to go your way – often the way of the Cross. I give you my eyes to see as you do. I give you my tongue to speak your words. I give you my mind that you may think in me. I give you my spirit that you may pray in me. I give you my heart that you may love in me, your Father and all people. I give you my whole self that you may grow in me, so that it is you, Lord Jesus, who live and work and pray in me.

For meditation
If anyone wants to be a follower of mine, let him renounce himself and take up his cross every day and follow me. (LUKE 9:23)

⊕
1 November: All Saints

GOSPEL READING: MATTHEW 5:1-12

REFLECTION

The saints have gone out of fashion! They are no longer venerated as in previous generations. Many of us never think about them and their influence in our lives unless we participate in the occasional novena in honour of a particular saint, for example, Saint Anthony when we lose something. Nevertheless the recent visit to Ireland and the United Kingdom of the relics of Saint Thérèse has reminded us that devotion to the saints is an important dimension of the practice of our Catholic faith.

Why does the Church teach us to believe in the communion of saints? Simply because, as Jesus teaches the crowds, their reward will be great in heaven if they live holy lives on this earth. In other words, holiness in this life brings success and happiness in the next life. Holiness is characterised by, among other virtues, being poor in spirit, being gentle, seeking justice, being merciful, making peace and enduring ill-treatment on account of the Good News. Saints are those people who, being faithful to the teaching of the Good News, have lived good lives. They have died in friendship with God.

It is tempting to assume that membership of the Church is confined solely to all people living on this earth who believe in Jesus Christ as their Saviour. However, the Church also includes the souls in purgatory. The souls in purgatory belong to those people who have died but who are not yet ready to be in perfect union with God in heaven because of their sins. The Church also includes the saints in heaven. We on earth are connected to both the souls in purgatory and the saints in heaven and we can pray for and inspire one another.

When we think about the saints, we often presume that they were extraordinary people who lived famous lives. But this is not always so. Saints are usually ordinary people living simple lives. In the words of Saint Thérèse, life is not about the extraordinary things we do. But it is about the ordinary things we do extraordinarily well. Christ's teaching challenges us to live ordinary lives extraordinarily well.

The primary message of the Feast of All Saints is that, like those who have gone before us from this life to the next life, we are called to be holy people in this life so that we can share in perfect happiness and union with God in heaven. The saints are models of Christian living that we can imitate. We are all called to be holy people, to be saints, and, like them, to live ordinary lives extraordinarily well. Let us bring the saints and their influence back into fashion! Let us strive for holiness so that, in the future, the Feast of All Saints will be our feast too.

For meditation

Rejoice and be glad, for your reward will be great in heaven; this is how they persecuted the prophets before you. (MATTHEW: 5:12)

⊕

2 November: Commemoration of
All the Faithful Departed

GOSPEL READING: LUKE 7:11-17

REFLECTION

As we approach the end of another Church year, we reflect on what has traditionally been called the four last things: death, judgement, heaven and hell. We remind ourselves again that life here on earth has one ultimate purpose: it provides us with the opportunities to prepare for the resurrection of the dead and eternal life.

Christians believe in the resurrection of the dead because of Christ's resurrection. What happened to him will happen to all people. We affirm our belief – although it does not always seem reasonable – that, while all life on this earth is terminal and while death is a fact of life, death is not the end for any of us. There is life after death, life that never ends. We believe that death in this life is the birth into eternal life. We live to die and, ironically, we die to live. This is the mystery of life and death. Therefore, in death life is changed, not ended.

God's plan is that all people will be in heaven for eternity. Nonetheless, God respects our free will and accepts how we use it. Therefore, our eternal destiny will depend on our choices in this life. Physical death is a consequence of sin. It marks the end of our personal existence and history. When we die our souls are separated from our bodies and eternity begins for us. We are then judged according to how we have lived in this world.

If our earthly lives have been completely faithful to the teaching of Christ and his Church, our souls will achieve eternal happiness in God's Blessed Presence in heaven and we will be numbered among the

Communion of Saints. If we have chosen instead to deny God and to ignore his call to conversion in Christ by living in a state of mortal sin, our souls will experience eternal alienation from God and hell will be our eternal destiny. However, if our lives have been sinful, but not to the extent that we have rejected God completely and deliberately, we will need purification so that, ultimately, we will become ready to be in God's Blessed Presence.

Traditionally during November, we pray for the souls in purgatory. Thus we pray for those who have died but whose souls are still in need of purification before they are ready to be with God in heaven for eternity. The Church's teaching about purgatory is very clear. Purgatory is an intermediate state in which the souls of the dead make amends for un-repented sins before receiving their eternal reward. Their release from purgatory is assisted by our prayers and penances. Hence the Church encourages us to pray for the dead always, but especially during November, commonly known as the Month of the Holy Souls. Significantly, the souls in purgatory pray for us.

The Catholic doctrine of purgatory is based on the Judaeo-Christian belief that praying for the dead is effective and to be commended. We intercede for those who have died because, as with all prayer, God listens and answers. Just as living believers in Jesus Christ are members of the Church, so too are the saints in heaven and the souls in purgatory. As such, the souls in purgatory can intercede for us. Knowing that they pray for us, we pray for them as we say: Eternal rest grant unto them, O Lord, and let perpetual light shine upon them. May they rest in peace. May their souls and the souls of all the faithful departed, through the mercy of God, rest in peace.

For meditation

*Everyone was filled with awe and praised God saying,
'A great prophet has appeared among us; God has
visited his people'.* (LUKE 7:16)

⊕
8 December: The Immaculate Conception
of the Blessed Virgin Mary

GOSPEL READING: LUKE 1:26-38

REFLECTION

The doctrine of the Immaculate Conception recognises
the sinlessness of Mary, the Mother of the Messiah, by
declaring that 'the Blessed Virgin Mary was preserved,
in the first instance of her conception, by a singular
grace and privilege of God omnipotent and because of
the merits of Jesus Christ the Saviour of the human
race, free from all stain of Original Sin' (from Pope Pius
IX's pronouncement of the dogma on 8 December
1854).

In the Book of Genesis, we read that sin first entered
the world through the disobedience of Adam and Eve
in the Garden of Eden. This sin, known as Original Sin,
seriously damaged the trusting relationship between
God and the human race and it is passed from one
generation to the next in every human conception. For
that reason, it was necessary that God undo its effects
by restoring the relationship to what it had been. He
did this by sending his Son into the world.

Through the angel Gabriel, God asked Mary to
cooperate in his plan of salvation by becoming the
Mother of his Son. Since she was going to give birth to
God's Son, it was appropriate that she would not be
tainted by sin and its consequences. Therefore, unlike

other human beings, she was redeemed at the moment of her conception by the utter holiness of Jesus (years before Jesus himself was born) in anticipation of the redemption from sin that would be won by him through his suffering and death on the cross.

The Catholic Church teaches that, because Jesus became incarnate of the Virgin Mary, it was proper that she be completely free of sin for consenting to become the Mother of the Saviour. The biblical account of the Annunciation records that the angel's greeting acknowledged Mary as being 'full of grace' or, as in the *Jerusalem Bible* translation, 'highly favoured' (Luke 1:28).

This does not mean that Mary did not have free will. She could have said 'No' to God's request but, instead, she said 'Yes'. She chose God just as God had chosen her. And it is her 'Yes' to God – in Latin, her *fiat* – that is her great example for the remainder of humankind. Mary's obedience to God was the complete opposite of the disobedience of Adam and Eve and, through that obedience, she repaired the damage done by Eve's disobedience. Interestingly, Saint Paul refers to Jesus as the Second Adam (see 1 Corinthians 15:21-22) and one of the most ancient titles of Mary is the Second Eve.

So Mary is a model of discipleship for all Christians. She was the first human being to gain the redemption won by her Son. As a strong but humble woman, ready to do God's will whatever the personal sacrifice, she is, pre-eminently, an inspiration for all of us. We hope and pray that, like Mary, we will benefit from the redemption won for us by her Son.

For meditation

You are to conceive and bear a son, and you must name him Jesus. (LUKE 1:31)

APPENDIX

Sunday 1	The Baptism of Jesus	Luke 3:15-16, 21-22
Sunday 2	The marriage feast at Cana	John 2:1-12
Sunday 3	Prologue. The visit to Nazareth (1)	Luke 1:1-4; 4:14-21
Sunday 4	The visit to Nazareth (2)	Luke 4:21-30
Sunday 5	* The call of the first apostles	Luke 5:1-11
Sunday 6	The sermon on the plain (1)	Luke 6:17, 20-26
Sunday 7	The sermon on the plain (2)	Luke 6:27-38
Sunday 8	The sermon on the plain (3)	Luke 6:39-45
Sunday 9	The cure of the centurion's servant	Luke 7:1-10
Sunday 10	* The widow of Nain	Luke 7:11-17
Sunday 11	* Jesus' feet anointed: the sinful woman	Luke 7:36–8:3
Sunday 12	Peter's confession of faith	Luke 9:18-24
Sunday 13	* The journey to Jerusalem begins	Luke 9:51-62
Sunday 14	* The mission of the seventy-two	Luke 10:1-12, 17-20
Sunday 15	* The parable of the good Samaritan	Luke 10:25-37
Sunday 16	* Martha and Mary	Luke 10:38-42
Sunday 17	* The importunate friend	Luke 11:1-13
Sunday 18	* The parable of the rich fool	Luke 12:13-21
Sunday 19	The need for vigilance	Luke 12:32-48
Sunday 20	'Not peace but division'	Luke 12:49-53
Sunday 21	Few will be saved	Luke 13:22-30
Sunday 22	True humility	Luke 14:1, 7-14
Sunday 23	The cost of discipleship	Luke 14:25-33
Sunday 24	*The parables of the lost coin, the lost sheep and the prodigal son	Luke 15:1-32
Sunday 25	* The parable of the unjust steward	Luke 16:1-13
Sunday 26	* The parable of the rich man and Lazarus	Luke 16:19-31
Sunday 27	* A lesson on faith and dedication	Luke 17:5-10
Sunday 28	* The ten lepers	Luke 17:11-19
Sunday 29	* The parable of the unjust judge	Luke 18:1-8
Sunday 30	* The parable of the Pharisee and the tax collector	Luke 18:9-14
Sunday 31	* Zacchaeus	Luke 19:1-10
Sunday 32	The resurrection debated	Luke 20:27-38
Sunday 33	The signs announcing the end	Luke 21:5-19
Sunday 34	* The repentant thief	Luke 23:35-43

Note: Passages marked with an asterisk are found only in the Gospel of Luke.